Tech of the Ancients

How Forgotten Innovations Continue to Influence Modern Technology

Ernesta Nieves

TECH OF THE ANCIENTS
© Copyright 2025 by Ernesta Nieves

All rights reserved

TABLE OF CONTENTS

Chapter 1: The Foundations of Innovation

The Dawn of Human Ingenuity

Human ingenuity traces its roots back to the moment early humans first sought to adapt their environment to their needs. Unlike other species that relied solely on instinct for survival, humans demonstrated a unique ability to observe, analyze, and manipulate the natural world in ways that would have lasting consequences for their development. This capacity for innovation began with small but profound steps, such as the creation of basic tools and the use of fire, which not only provided warmth and protection but also expanded dietary possibilities through cooking. These early advancements set the foundation for a trajectory of technological and cultural evolution that continues to shape our lives today.

The earliest tools fashioned by human ancestors were simple yet transformative. Stones chipped to create sharp edges became the first rudimentary cutting instruments, allowing early humans to process food, hunt more effectively, and defend themselves from predators. These tools, often referred to as Oldowan tools, date back more than two million years and represent the dawn of deliberate craftsmanship. Through trial and error, early humans discovered the best materials for toolmaking, favoring harder stones like flint and obsidian for their durability and sharpness. This practice illustrated a fundamental principle of ingenuity: the ability to learn from experience and refine methods over time.

Fire, another pivotal discovery, marked a turning point in human history. Beyond its immediate practical uses, such as providing warmth and deterring predators, fire had profound effects on human biology and society. Cooked food is easier to digest, allowing for better nutrient absorption, which likely contributed to the development of larger brains over generations. Fire also extended the day, enabling social interactions and storytelling around communal hearths, fostering a sense of community and shared knowledge. The controlled use of fire required observation and experimentation, underscoring the importance of curiosity and perseverance in the process of innovation.

Observation played a critical role in early human ingenuity. By closely studying their surroundings, early humans gleaned insights into patterns and relationships within the natural world. They noticed, for instance, that certain plants could be used for medicinal purposes, while others were toxic. They observed the behaviors of animals to improve hunting strategies and recognized the cyclical nature of seasons, which later informed agricultural practices. This ability to observe and make connections laid the groundwork for more complex innovations, as it encouraged a mindset of exploration and problem-solving.

Trial and error were equally vital in the evolution of early inventions. Mistakes were not merely setbacks but opportunities for learning. When an attempt to create a particular tool or structure failed, early humans adjusted their methods until they achieved success. This iterative process of experimentation and adaptation is a hallmark of human ingenuity, evident not only in the past but also in the technological advancements of today. It reflects an inherent resilience and determination to overcome challenges, traits that have driven progress throughout history.

The foundational innovations of early humans were not just isolated achievements but stepping stones that enabled more sophisticated developments. The creation of tools led to the construction of shelters, the development of clothing, and the invention of weapons for hunting and defense. The mastery of fire paved the way for metallurgy, as early humans discovered that certain rocks, when exposed to high heat, could be transformed into malleable metals. These cascading advancements demonstrate how one innovation often serves as a catalyst for others, creating a ripple effect that propels societies forward.

While these early accomplishments may seem distant and rudimentary compared to modern technology, their underlying principles remain relevant. The ability to observe, experiment, and adapt continues to drive innovation in fields ranging from medicine to engineering. By studying the ingenuity of early humans, we gain a deeper appreciation for the resourcefulness and creativity that define our species. It is a reminder that even the most complex technologies of today owe their existence to the simple, yet profound, innovations of the past.

Early Tools and Their Timeless Principles

The creation of early tools stands as one of humanity's most transformative milestones, marking the moment when intellect began to shape the physical world with purpose. These tools, rudimentary by modern standards, carry principles that remain deeply embedded in technology and engineering. They were not merely instruments to solve immediate problems, but embodiments of observation, adaptation, and creativity that have echoed throughout the centuries. Early humans, driven by necessity and survival, forged the first connections between thought and action, creating objects that amplified their abilities, extended their reach, and ultimately changed the trajectory of human existence.

The earliest tools were crafted with a simplicity that belied their profound impact. Stones were shaped into cutting edges, their sharp surfaces used to slice through animal hide, butcher meat, or carve wood. These were not random stones picked up and used in their natural state but pieces deliberately selected and manipulated to serve a purpose. The process of flaking one stone against another to create a sharp edge signaled a leap in cognitive ability—an understanding of cause and effect, of materials and their properties, and of an object's usefulness when it was altered. These early tools, such as Oldowan and Acheulean hand axes, were far more than just objects; they were physical manifestations of ingenuity and problem-solving.

The principle at the heart of these tools was efficiency. A sharp-edged stone could perform tasks that bare hands or teeth could not, conserving energy and time, which were vital commodities in the harsh environments of early human life. This pursuit of efficiency remains a core driver of innovation today, whether in creating more fuel-efficient engines or designing algorithms to process vast amounts of data. The same principle that guided the shaping of a stone tool guides modern engineers and inventors in their quest to make processes faster, easier, and more effective. Another enduring principle embedded in early tools is adaptability. As humans spread across diverse landscapes, they encountered new challenges and environments, requiring them to modify their tools to meet varying demands. In regions where stone was scarce, other materials such as bone or wood were used. This adaptability demonstrated an understanding of the resources available and the ability to repurpose them creatively. This same mindset is reflected in modern technology, where materials and designs are constantly adapted to suit specific needs, from lightweight alloys in aerospace engineering to biodegradable plastics in sustainability efforts.

Collaboration also played a crucial role in the development of early tools. The sharing of knowledge within small groups allowed for the refinement of designs and techniques. A toolmaker who discovered a better method of flint knapping could pass that knowledge to others, creating a ripple effect of improvement. This communal aspect of innovation reveals that technology has never been a solitary endeavor. From the exchange of ideas in ancient toolmaking communities to the global networks of researchers and engineers today, collaboration remains a key principle driving progress.

Durability was another hallmark of early tools, as they needed to withstand repeated use in demanding conditions. A poorly made tool that broke easily could mean the difference between survival and failure. Thus, early humans learned to select materials and refine their techniques to create objects that could endure. The emphasis on durability persists in modern design, where products are often judged by their reliability and longevity, from bridges that must endure for centuries to smartphones that must survive daily wear and tear.

The influence of early tools extends beyond their physical form to the way they shaped human behavior and thought. The act of creating a tool required planning and foresight, as well as an understanding of how the tool would interact with its intended environment. This ability to project future outcomes based on present actions was a critical cognitive leap, laying the groundwork for more complex forms of problem-solving and innovation. The very process of toolmaking also nurtured patience and persistence, qualities that remain essential for overcoming obstacles in any creative endeavor.

Early tools also began to blur the line between humanity and its environment. By using tools, humans extended their physical capabilities, transforming themselves into beings that could hunt larger prey, manipulate tougher materials, and survive in harsher climates. Tools became extensions of the human body, amplifying strength, precision, and efficiency. This concept of amplification has only grown more sophisticated over time, from the levers and pulleys of classical mechanics to the digital tools of the information age. Yet, the underlying principle remains unchanged—the desire to transcend natural limitations through ingenuity.

The legacy of early tools is not confined to their immediate utility. They were the first step in a continuum of innovation that would lead to the construction of shelters, the creation of art, and the development of agriculture. Each subsequent achievement built upon the foundation laid by these simple yet profound objects. The principles they embodied— efficiency, adaptability, collaboration, durability, and foresight—became the bedrock of technological advancement, guiding humanity as it ventured into increasingly complex realms of invention.

Even as modern tools and technologies evolve at an unprecedented pace, the lessons of early tools remain relevant. They remind us that progress is rooted in understanding the materials and forces of the world around us, in adapting to challenges with creativity and resilience, and in working together to refine and improve our efforts. The ingenuity of early humans, expressed through the crafting of the first tools, continues to resonate as a testament to the timeless principles that drive innovation.

The Role of Observation in Ancient Problem-Solving

Observation, as one of humanity's earliest and most powerful tools, has always been integral to problem-solving. Long before written records or systematic scientific processes, ancient humans relied on their senses and critical thinking to navigate the challenges of survival and to thrive in their environments. By closely studying the natural world, they uncovered patterns, developed strategies, and crafted solutions that often defied the limitations imposed by their circumstances. This ability to observe and interpret the world around them not only addressed immediate concerns but also laid the groundwork for more advanced technologies and innovations that would emerge over time.

The natural environment served as both a canvas and a teacher for ancient humans. For early hunter-gatherers, survival depended on an acute awareness of their surroundings. They observed the behavior of animals to predict migration patterns, identify potential predators, and refine their hunting strategies. By noting the habits of prey, such as when and where certain animals gathered to drink water, they could anticipate opportunities for successful hunts. This intimate understanding of animal behavior evolved into techniques that allowed humans to become more efficient hunters, using tools and traps that were designed with these observations in mind. Such focused attention to detail was not born from instinct but from a cultivated practice of learning and adapting, traits that would define the trajectory of human progress.

The landscape itself also revealed valuable lessons to those who paid close attention. The movement of the sun, the phases of the moon, and the changing constellations in the night sky allowed early humans to track time and seasons. This knowledge was essential for understanding planting cycles, preparing for migration, or predicting weather changes. Observing how water flowed through valleys led to the identification of fertile land for agriculture, while the behavior of rivers taught valuable lessons about flooding and irrigation. This attentiveness to natural phenomena eventually gave rise to some of the earliest known agricultural societies, as humans began to manipulate their environment based on what they had learned. Observation turned necessity into opportunity, allowing humans to move from reactive survival to proactive planning.

Beyond the physical world, humans also observed their own interactions and the dynamics within their communities. Ancient problem-solving often required collaboration, and understanding how individuals worked together was critical. They noted the importance of shared effort in tasks like building shelters, hunting large game, or defending against external threats. This social awareness helped foster cooperation, division of labor, and the eventual development of complex societal structures. Over time, these observations of human behavior contributed to the creation of governing rules, cultural norms, and systems of communication that enhanced group cohesion and efficiency.

The role of observation extended into early medicine, where it became a cornerstone of healing practices. Ancient healers, often guided by trial and error, paid close attention to the effects of various plants, roots, and minerals on the human body. They noted which herbs alleviated pain, which berries were poisonous, and which concoctions could reduce fever or inflammation. In Mesopotamia, Egypt, and later in Greece, the careful study of symptoms and their progression allowed for the development of rudimentary medical practices. Observing how wounds healed or failed to heal led to basic sanitation techniques, such as washing injuries or applying antiseptic substances like honey. These practices, rooted in meticulous observation, formed the basis of what would eventually become modern medicine.

One of the most striking examples of observational problem-solving can be seen in ancient engineering and construction. The builders of the Egyptian pyramids, for instance, relied on keen observations of geometry, balance, and material properties to construct monuments that have endured for thousands of years. By studying the properties of stone, they understood how to cut and transport massive blocks with precision. Similarly, ancient Mesopotamians observed the behavior of clay when exposed to heat, leading to the invention of bricks that could be used for more durable structures. Observation allowed these civilizations to push the boundaries of what was thought possible, creating architectural marvels that still inspire awe today.

Observation also played a key role in the development of early tools and machines. The Archimedes screw, for example, is thought to have been inspired by observing how water moved naturally through certain formations or patterns. Early inventors noted the principles of leverage, friction, and force by watching how everyday objects behaved under different conditions. These insights were then applied to create devices that amplified human capability, from simple levers and pulleys to more intricate mechanisms like the Antikythera device. Each invention was a testament to the power of looking closely at the world and uncovering the hidden principles that governed it.

Even in the spiritual and philosophical realms, observation was a guiding force. Early civilizations frequently looked to the heavens for guidance, interpreting celestial movements as messages from the divine or as markers of natural cycles. The Mayans, for instance, developed highly accurate calendars by observing the stars, while ancient Chinese scholars used celestial patterns to predict eclipses. These observations were not merely acts of wonder but practical tools for organizing agricultural schedules, planning religious ceremonies, and understanding humanity's place within the cosmos.

The importance of observation in ancient problem-solving cannot be overstated. It was a skill that required patience, attention to detail, and a willingness to learn from failure. The lessons gleaned from the natural world, from human behavior, and from the interaction between the two informed nearly every aspect of early human life. These observations laid the foundations for agriculture, medicine, engineering, and even governance. They transformed uncertainty into knowledge and chaos into order, setting the stage for humanity's enduring quest to understand and shape the world. Observing with intention and purpose remains as relevant now as it was then, a timeless principle that continues to drive discovery and innovation.

Trial, Error, and the Evolution of Early Inventions

The evolution of early inventions was rarely a straight path but one characterized by countless attempts, missteps, and the enduring resilience of trial and error. This process—marked by experimentation, failure, and eventual success—revealed the innate determination of early humans to overcome challenges and adapt their environment to their needs. Each failure became a lesson, and each success a building block, as ancient humans refined their tools, techniques, and understanding of the natural world. Trial and error was not merely a method of solving problems; it was the engine of innovation that propelled humanity forward.

When early humans first began shaping stones into tools, it was not an act of immediate mastery. The process of flaking a stone into a sharp edge required precision, practice, and a recognition of what worked and what did not. A poorly struck blow could shatter the stone, rendering it useless, while a carefully considered strike could create a functional cutting edge. Over time, these early toolmakers learned which types of stone were best suited for their needs, favoring materials like flint and obsidian for their durability and sharpness. This knowledge was not acquired in a single moment of inspiration but through repeated trials, each failure teaching something new about the properties of the materials and the techniques required to shape them.

The principle of trial and error extended beyond tools to the development of fire. Early humans likely discovered fire by observing natural phenomena such as lightning strikes or volcanic eruptions, but learning to create and control it was a far more complex endeavor. The act of striking flint against steel or rubbing sticks together to produce sparks would have required countless attempts. Even the smallest success—a faint ember or a wisp of smoke—would have spurred further experimentation, leading to the eventual mastery of fire-making. This achievement transformed human life, providing warmth, protection, and the ability to cook food, all of which contributed to health and social cohesion. It was trial and error that unlocked the potential of fire, turning a natural force into a tool of survival and progress.

Agriculture, another cornerstone of human advancement, was similarly born from experimentation. The transition from hunting and gathering to farming was not an instant shift but a gradual process of observation and adaptation. Early humans began to notice that seeds dropped near their settlements would sometimes sprout and grow into plants. Acting on this observation, they began to deliberately plant seeds, experimenting with different types of crops and methods of cultivation. Failures were inevitable—some seeds failed to germinate, and others were destroyed by pests or drought—but each setback provided valuable insights. Over generations, these early farmers developed techniques such as crop rotation, irrigation, and soil management, all of which were products of trial and error. This iterative process transformed the way humans interacted with the land, laying the foundation for settled communities and the rise of civilizations.

The construction of shelters also demonstrates the role of trial and error in early innovation. The first attempts to create protective structures were likely rudimentary, involving the use of branches, leaves, and other available materials. These early shelters may have collapsed under their own weight or failed to withstand harsh weather, but each failure prompted adjustments and improvements. Over time, humans learned to incorporate stronger materials like stone and clay, as well as architectural principles such as support beams and angled roofs for water drainage. These advancements were not the result of a single moment of inspiration but of countless iterations, each one building on the lessons of the past.

Water management, essential for both survival and the development of agriculture, also emerged through a process of trial and error. Early humans observed how water flowed naturally through the landscape, carving paths through valleys and pooling in low-lying areas. They experimented with ways to redirect and store water, creating rudimentary channels and reservoirs. Some of these early attempts may have failed, leading to flooding or water loss, but each mistake provided new insights into the behavior of water and the materials used to contain it. Over time, these efforts evolved into sophisticated irrigation systems, such as those seen in ancient Mesopotamia and Egypt, where canals and aqueducts were used to transport water over long distances. These systems not only supported agriculture but also enabled the growth of cities, demonstrating how trial and error could lead to transformative innovations.

The iterative nature of invention also fostered a culture of resilience and perseverance. Early humans understood that failure was not the end of the process but an integral part of it. Each unsuccessful attempt was a step closer to success, a concept that remains central to innovation today. This mindset encouraged a willingness to take risks and explore new possibilities, qualities that were essential for navigating the uncertainties of the ancient world. Whether crafting a tool, building a shelter, or cultivating crops, early humans approached each challenge with curiosity and determination, using trial and error as a means of discovery and refinement. The lessons of trial and error are as relevant now as they were in the past. They remind us that progress is rarely linear and that failure is not a sign of defeat but an opportunity for growth. The resilience and resourcefulness demonstrated by early humans have left an enduring legacy, shaping the way we approach problems and seek solutions. Their willingness to experiment, learn from mistakes, and persist in the face of challenges laid the foundation for the countless innovations that followed. It is through this process of trial and error that humanity has continued to evolve, turning obstacles into opportunities and ideas into reality.

How Ancient Foundations Shape Modern Engineering

Th engineering marvels of the modern world stand on the shoulders of ancient innovations, many of which established principles still in use today. The structures, tools, and systems developed in antiquity were not merely solutions for survival or convenience—they were expressions of ingenuity and foresight, laying the groundwork for disciplines that would evolve over millennia. From the towering pyramids to the elegant arches of Roman aqueducts, the foundations laid by ancient engineers continue to influence the way we build, innovate, and solve problems in the present day.

One of the most enduring legacies of ancient engineering is the understanding of materials and their properties. Ancient builders were keen observers of the natural world, carefully selecting materials based on their unique characteristics. They recognized the strength of limestone and granite, the malleability of metals like bronze and copper, and the insulating properties of clay. The Great Pyramid of Giza, for example, stands as a testament to this understanding. Constructed using massive limestone blocks, the pyramid demonstrates an early mastery of quarrying, transportation, and assembly techniques. Modern engineering still relies on this foundational knowledge, with material science remaining a cornerstone of construction, aerospace, and manufacturing industries. The ability to analyze and manipulate materials, pioneered by ancient civilizations, has allowed us to create everything from skyscrapers to spacecraft.

The principles of load distribution and structural integrity, first explored by ancient builders, also remain central to modern engineering. The use of arches and domes, perfected by the Romans, revolutionized architecture by providing a way to distribute weight evenly across a structure. The Colosseum, with its intricate network of arches, is a prime example of this innovation. The design allowed for the construction of massive, stable structures that could support significant loads while conserving materials. Today, these same principles are used in the construction of bridges, tunnels, and stadiums, proving that the insights of ancient engineers were not only revolutionary in their time but timeless in their application.

Water management systems developed in antiquity were another critical foundation for modern engineering. Civilizations such as the Mesopotamians, Greeks, and Romans understood the importance of controlling and distributing water for agriculture, sanitation, and urban development. The aqueducts of Rome, which transported water over vast distances using a combination of gravity and carefully calculated gradients, remain a marvel of engineering precision. These systems not only supplied cities with fresh water but also inspired the development of modern plumbing and irrigation techniques. The ability to manage water efficiently, a skill honed by ancient engineers, continues to be a vital aspect of urban planning and environmental sustainability.

Ancient road networks, particularly those of the Roman Empire, demonstrate an early understanding of connectivity and infrastructure. Roman roads were meticulously constructed, with layers of stone, gravel, and sand designed to provide stability and drainage. This attention to detail ensured that the roads could withstand heavy use and adverse weather conditions, enabling the movement of armies, goods, and information across vast territories. The concept of durable, well-maintained transportation networks remains a cornerstone of modern engineering, with highways, railways, and air traffic systems all drawing inspiration from the principles established by ancient road builders.

The influence of ancient engineering extends beyond physical structures to encompass systems and processes. The use of levers, pulleys, and gears, first explored by inventors like Archimedes, laid the groundwork for mechanical engineering. These simple machines, which amplified human effort and efficiency, are still used in countless applications today, from cranes and elevators to complex robotics. The understanding of mechanical advantage, a concept first articulated in antiquity, continues to drive innovation in fields ranging from automotive design to renewable energy.

Sustainability, a pressing concern in contemporary engineering, also has its roots in ancient practices. Many ancient civilizations understood the importance of working in harmony with the environment, using resources judiciously and designing systems that minimized waste. The city of Petra, carved into the sandstone cliffs of modern-day Jordan, is a striking example of sustainable engineering. Its builders designed an intricate system of channels, cisterns, and reservoirs to capture and store water in an arid climate, ensuring the city's survival for centuries. Today, engineers and urban planners look to such examples for inspiration as they develop sustainable solutions to modern challenges, from water scarcity to climate change.

Ancient engineering was not limited to grand monuments or large-scale infrastructure; it also encompassed everyday innovations that improved quality of life. The development of mills for grinding grain, the use of wind and water power, and the construction of kilns for pottery and metallurgy all demonstrate a deep understanding of physics and efficiency. These small-scale technologies, while often overshadowed by more monumental achievements, were equally important in shaping the trajectory of human development. They exemplify how ancient engineers applied their knowledge to practical problems, creating tools and systems that would influence generations to come.

Perhaps the most profound contribution of ancient engineering lies in its ability to inspire. The ingenuity and ambition of ancient builders remind us of what is possible when creativity, knowledge, and determination converge. The legacy of ancient engineering is not merely a collection of techniques and principles but a testament to the human capacity for innovation. It challenges modern engineers to think beyond the constraints of the present, to draw on the lessons of the past, and to envision solutions that will stand the test of time.

The foundations laid by ancient engineers continue to shape the world in ways both tangible and intangible. Their achievements remind us that progress is built layer by layer, each generation adding to the knowledge and accomplishments of those who came before. The principles of material science, structural integrity, water management, connectivity, and sustainability, first explored in antiquity, remain as relevant today as they were thousands of years ago. By studying and building upon these ancient foundations, modern engineering not only honors the past but also ensures a future of continued innovation and discovery.

Chapter 2: Architectural Marvels and Structural Ingenuity

The Secrets of the Pyramids

The pyramids of ancient Egypt stand as some of the most extraordinary architectural achievements in human history. These structures, monumental in scale and breathtaking in precision, have captured the imagination of countless generations. They are more than mere tombs for the pharaohs who commissioned them; they represent the culmination of advanced engineering, societal organization, and a profound understanding of mathematics and materials. The secrets of their construction, though studied extensively, still inspire awe and speculation, as they reveal the ingenuity and ambition of their creators.

The Great Pyramid of Giza, built for Pharaoh Khufu around 4,500 years ago, remains the most iconic of these architectural wonders. Rising to a height of nearly 146 meters (originally, before erosion and the loss of its outer casing stones), it was the tallest man-made structure in the world for over 3,800 years. Its construction required the movement and placement of approximately 2.3 million blocks of limestone and granite, some weighing as much as 80 tons. How such massive materials were quarried, transported, and assembled with such precision in an era devoid of modern machinery has been the subject of extensive research and debate.

The first step in constructing the pyramids was meticulous planning. The builders had to select a site that could support the immense weight of the structure and provide easy access to the necessary materials. The Giza plateau, with its solid limestone bedrock, offered an ideal foundation. Its proximity to the Nile River also allowed for the transportation of massive stone blocks from distant quarries. Recent studies suggest that a network of canals may have been dug to bring the stones closer to the construction site, a logistical innovation that underscores the importance of water transport in ancient engineering.

One of the most remarkable aspects of the pyramids is their alignment with celestial bodies. The Great Pyramid, for instance, is aligned almost perfectly with the cardinal points of the compass. This precision indicates that the ancient Egyptians possessed a sophisticated understanding of astronomy and geometry. It is thought that they used the stars to determine true north, a technique that would have required careful observation and calculation. The alignment not only reflects their engineering prowess but also their deep spiritual beliefs, as the pyramids were designed to connect the earthly realm with the heavens, ensuring the pharaoh's journey to the afterlife.

The construction process itself remains a topic of fascination and debate. Theories about how the massive stones were moved and lifted into place range from the use of sledges and ramps to more speculative ideas involving counterweights or even lost technologies. The most widely accepted theory involves a system of ramps, either straight, zigzagging, or circular, that allowed workers to haul the stones to the desired height. These ramps would have required constant adjustment and maintenance as the pyramid rose, demonstrating an incredible level of coordination and manpower.

The workforce responsible for building the pyramids has often been romanticized as slaves toiling under brutal conditions, but modern archaeological evidence suggests otherwise. Excavations near the Giza pyramids have uncovered workers' villages, complete with barracks, bakeries, and medical facilities. These findings indicate that the laborers were skilled craftsmen and farmers conscripted during the agricultural off-season, well-fed and cared for to ensure their productivity. The scale of this operation highlights the organizational capabilities of the ancient Egyptian state, which could mobilize and manage thousands of workers over decades.

The materials used in the pyramids further illustrate the ingenuity of their builders. The core of the Great Pyramid is composed of locally quarried limestone, while the outer casing, now mostly lost, was made of highly polished Tura limestone that reflected sunlight, giving the pyramid a dazzling appearance. The inner chambers and passageways, meanwhile, were constructed using granite blocks transported from Aswan, located over 800 kilometers away. These granite blocks, used for their strength and durability, were shaped with remarkable precision, fitting together so tightly that even a blade of grass could not pass between them. The ability to quarry, transport, and position such materials speaks to the advanced tools and techniques at the Egyptians' disposal.

The internal structure of the pyramids is equally impressive. The Great Pyramid contains a series of chambers and passageways, including the King's Chamber, the Queen's Chamber, and the enigmatic Grand Gallery. These spaces were constructed with careful attention to both function and symbolism. The King's Chamber, for instance, is lined with massive granite blocks and features a flat ceiling supported by a series of "relieving chambers" above it, designed to distribute weight and prevent collapse. This ingenious solution demonstrates a sophisticated understanding of structural engineering and load-bearing principles.

The purpose of the pyramids extends beyond their architectural and engineering achievements. They were deeply connected to the religious and cultural beliefs of ancient Egypt. The pyramid's shape, thought to represent the rays of the sun, symbolized the pharaoh's ascent to join the sun god Ra in the afterlife. The internal layout, with narrow shafts aligned to specific stars, further emphasized this celestial connection. The pyramids were not just tombs but gateways to eternity, designed to ensure the pharaoh's immortality and, by extension, the stability and prosperity of the kingdom.

Despite centuries of study, the pyramids continue to guard some of their secrets. Questions remain about the exact methods of construction, the tools used, and the full extent of their symbolic meaning. New technologies, such as ground-penetrating radar and thermal imaging, have revealed previously unknown voids and anomalies within the Great Pyramid, hinting at hidden chambers or passageways yet to be explored. Each discovery adds to our understanding of these ancient marvels while deepening the mystery that surrounds them.

The pyramids of Egypt stand as enduring monuments to human ingenuity, ambition, and the desire to leave a legacy that transcends time. They remind us of what can be achieved through careful planning, collaboration, and a deep understanding of the natural world. As we continue to uncover their secrets, we gain not only insights into the engineering brilliance of the ancient Egyptians but also a greater appreciation for the timeless quest to create something extraordinary.

Roman Concrete: A Lost Recipe Rediscovered

Roman concrete, known as opus caementicium, stands as one of the most remarkable achievements of ancient engineering. Its resilience and versatility allowed the Romans to construct an array of architectural masterpieces, many of which still endure today. From the grandeur of the Pantheon to the aqueducts that carried water across vast distances, Roman concrete revolutionized construction and left an indelible mark on architectural history. The ingenuity behind this material was not merely a matter of convenience or practicality; it was a deliberate and sophisticated response to the challenges of building structures that could withstand time, weather, and even seismic activity. Yet, for centuries, the precise formula and methods used to create Roman concrete were shrouded in mystery, only recently rediscovered through modern research.

The key ingredients of Roman concrete were lime, volcanic ash, and rubble or aggregate. While lime and aggregate were commonly used in other ancient building materials, it was the inclusion of volcanic ash that set Roman concrete apart. This ash, particularly the variety known as pozzolana, was sourced from regions such as the Bay of Naples. When mixed with lime and water, the volcanic ash triggered a chemical reaction that formed calcium-silicate-hydrate crystals, binding the mixture into a robust, cohesive material. Unlike modern Portland cement, which hardens quickly but is prone to cracking over time, Roman concrete grew stronger with age due to its unique chemical composition.

One of the most striking features of Roman concrete was its ability to set underwater, a property that allowed the construction of harbors, piers, and other maritime structures. This hydraulic capability was achieved by combining lime with volcanic ash rich in aluminosilicates. The chemical reaction that occurred when the mixture came into contact with water created a durable material that could withstand the corrosive effects of saltwater. Roman engineers exploited this property to expand their empire's naval infrastructure, including the construction of ports such as Caesarea Maritima in modern-day Israel. The durability of these underwater structures, some of which have survived for over two millennia, is a testament to the advanced understanding of materials possessed by Roman builders.

The versatility of Roman concrete enabled the construction of architectural forms that had previously been unimaginable. The Pantheon in Rome, with its massive unreinforced concrete dome, remains one of the most extraordinary examples of this ingenuity. The dome, which spans 43.3 meters in diameter, was achieved by gradually reducing the weight of the concrete mixture as the structure rose. Heavier aggregates were used at the base, while lighter materials such as pumice were incorporated near the top. This gradient of materials not only reduced the overall weight of the dome but also distributed stress evenly, ensuring its stability. The oculus at the dome's center, a circular opening that allows light to pour into the interior, further reduced weight while adding a dramatic visual effect. The Pantheon's longevity and structural integrity are direct results of the careful application of Roman concrete's properties.

Aqueducts, another hallmark of Roman engineering, also benefited from the use of concrete. These monumental structures, designed to transport water over long distances, required both strength and flexibility to traverse varied terrains. Concrete allowed for the construction of arches and vaults, which distributed weight efficiently and minimized the need for additional support. The Pont du Gard in southern France, a towering aqueduct that spans the Gardon River, exemplifies how concrete enabled the Romans to achieve both functionality and aesthetic beauty. The use of concrete not only simplified construction but also ensured that these critical infrastructures could endure centuries of use.

Despite its widespread use and remarkable durability, the knowledge of how to produce Roman concrete faded with the decline of the Roman Empire. As Europe entered the Middle Ages, the techniques and materials that had enabled the construction of such enduring structures were largely forgotten. Builders reverted to using less durable materials, and the architectural achievements of Rome became objects of admiration rather than models to emulate. It was not until the modern era that engineers and scientists began to study Roman concrete in earnest, seeking to uncover the secrets of its longevity.

Recent analyses of Roman concrete samples have revealed fascinating insights into its composition and performance. Using advanced techniques such as scanning electron microscopy and X-ray diffraction, researchers have identified the crystalline structures that form within the material over time. One particularly significant discovery is the presence of a rare mineral called tobermorite. This mineral, which forms through the reaction between lime and volcanic ash, plays a crucial role in reinforcing the concrete and preventing cracks from spreading. Unlike modern concrete, which is prone to deterioration when exposed to water, Roman concrete's ability to self-heal through chemical reactions has contributed to its remarkable durability.

The rediscovery of Roman concrete has sparked renewed interest in its potential applications in modern construction. In an era when sustainability and resilience are paramount, the advantages of this ancient material are particularly compelling. The production of modern cement is a significant source of carbon dioxide emissions, accounting for nearly 8% of global emissions. By contrast, the production of Roman concrete required lower temperatures and incorporated naturally occurring materials, resulting in a smaller environmental footprint. Researchers are now exploring how the principles of Roman concrete can be adapted to create more sustainable building materials, combining ancient wisdom with modern technology.

The legacy of Roman concrete extends far beyond the structures it was used to build. It represents a profound understanding of materials science, an ability to innovate in response to practical challenges, and a vision of architecture as a lasting expression of human ingenuity. The rediscovery of its secrets not only deepens our appreciation for the achievements of the past but also offers valuable lessons for the future. As we face the challenges of building resilient, sustainable infrastructure in a rapidly changing world, the wisdom of the Romans serves as both a guide and an inspiration. Their ability to create something so enduring reminds us that the solutions to modern problems often lie in the ingenuity of history.

The Precision of Ancient City Planning

The precision of ancient city planning reveals a level of sophistication and foresight that continues to influence modern urban design. Far from being a series of haphazard settlements, many ancient cities were meticulously designed to meet the needs of their inhabitants while reflecting cultural, political, and spiritual priorities. These early planners considered factors such as geography, resources, defense, and social organization, creating urban environments that were both functional and symbolic. Their achievements not only provided a blueprint for urban living but also demonstrated a deep understanding of human behavior and the natural world.

One of the most striking examples of ancient city planning is found in the Indus Valley Civilization, which flourished around 2500 BCE in what is now Pakistan and northwest India. Cities like Mohenjo-Daro and Harappa were laid out with remarkable precision, featuring a grid-like pattern that rivaled modern urban layouts. Streets were aligned at right angles, creating a series of carefully organized blocks. This systematic approach allowed for efficient movement and access, ensuring that residents could navigate their city with ease. Such planning required not only advanced surveying techniques but also a clear vision of how to balance public and private spaces.

The infrastructure of Indus Valley cities further highlights their planners' ingenuity. Drainage systems ran beneath the streets, channeling wastewater away from homes and public spaces. Many houses were equipped with private wells and bathing areas, reflecting an emphasis on hygiene and public health. The integration of water management into the urban fabric was both practical and revolutionary, ensuring that the cities could support large populations while minimizing the risk of disease. These systems demonstrate a level of engineering expertise that was unparalleled for its time and would not be seen again in many parts of the world for centuries. Ancient Egypt also showcased extraordinary city planning, driven largely by the central authority of the pharaohs. Cities like Thebes and Memphis were designed with a clear hierarchy in mind, reflecting the stratified nature of Egyptian society. Temples and palaces occupied prominent positions, often aligned with celestial phenomena or natural landmarks such as the Nile River. This alignment was not merely aesthetic; it was deeply symbolic, reinforcing the connection between the divine, the natural world, and the ruling class. Surrounding these monumental structures were residential areas, which were often organized according to social status. The deliberate placement of structures within the city underscored the importance of order and balance, principles that were central to Egyptian cosmology.

In ancient Greece, city planning took on a more human-centered approach, emphasizing the relationship between the individual and the community. The concept of the polis, or city-state, was central to Greek identity, and cities like Athens and Miletus were designed to foster civic engagement. Public spaces such as the agora served as hubs for commerce, debate, and social interaction, while theaters and gymnasiums provided venues for cultural and physical pursuits. The layout of these cities was often influenced by the natural landscape, with planners integrating hills, rivers, and coastlines into their designs. This harmony between the built and natural environments reflected the Greek ideal of moderation and balance, ensuring that cities were not only functional but also inspiring.

The Romans, inheriting and expanding upon Greek principles, brought city planning to an unprecedented level of complexity and standardization. The castrum, a type of Roman military camp, served as the prototype for many Roman cities. These camps were laid out in a grid pattern, with two main streets, the cardo and decumanus, intersecting at a central forum. This design provided a clear and logical structure, making it easy to navigate and administer. As the Roman Empire expanded, this template was applied to cities across Europe, North Africa, and the Middle East, creating a sense of uniformity and cohesion within the empire.

Roman cities were also remarkable for their infrastructure, which supported both practicality and luxury. Aqueducts supplied fresh water, while sewer systems ensured sanitation. Roads, often paved with stone, connected cities to one another, facilitating trade and communication. Public buildings such as baths, amphitheaters, and temples were strategically placed to serve the population while enhancing the city's aesthetic appeal. This integration of utility and grandeur reflected the Roman belief in the city as a microcosm of their civilization, a place where order, culture, and power converged.

In ancient China, city planning was deeply influenced by philosophical and cosmological principles. The ideal city was seen as a reflection of the universe, with its layout designed to align with cardinal directions and cosmic forces. The ancient capital of Chang'an, for example, was built according to a strict grid pattern based on the principles of feng shui and Confucian ideals. The city's walls, gates, and avenues were carefully placed to ensure harmony between human activity and the natural world. At the heart of Chang'an was the imperial palace, symbolizing the central role of the emperor as the mediator between heaven and earth. This integration of spiritual and practical considerations created cities that were as much expressions of philosophy as they were centers of governance.

Mesoamerican civilizations such as the Maya and the Aztecs also demonstrated remarkable city planning. Cities like Tikal and Tenochtitlan were designed to accommodate large populations while reflecting the religious and cultural values of their societies. Tenochtitlan, the capital of the Aztec Empire, was built on an island in Lake Texcoco, accessible by a network of causeways and canals. This unique setting required innovative solutions for transportation, water management, and agriculture, including the creation of chinampas, or floating gardens. The city's layout, with its central temple complex and surrounding residential areas, emphasized the importance of religion and community in Aztec life.

The precision and creativity of ancient city planning reveal not only technical skill but also a profound understanding of the needs and aspirations of their inhabitants. These cities were more than collections of buildings; they were carefully crafted environments that facilitated trade, governance, worship, and social interaction. Their planners balanced practicality with symbolism, creating spaces that were functional, beautiful, and deeply connected to the values of their time.

The legacy of ancient city planning continues to shape the way we approach urban design today. Concepts such as zoning, public spaces, and infrastructure owe much to the innovations of the past. By studying these ancient cities, we gain insight into the enduring principles of effective planning and the ways in which built environments can reflect and enhance human society. Their achievements remind us that thoughtful design is not merely a technical exercise but a profound expression of culture, vision, and humanity's desire to create order and meaning in the world.

Monumental Structures That Defy Time

Monumental structures from ancient civilizations stand today as enduring testaments to human ambition, ingenuity, and the desire to create something that lasts beyond the fleeting span of individual lives. These edifices, built with precision and purpose, not only served practical or ceremonial functions in their time but also carried messages of power, spirituality, and identity. Their survival across millennia, often in the face of natural disasters, wars, and the relentless wear of time, highlights the extraordinary skill and vision of the architects and builders who conceived them. These monumental structures, whether temples, tombs, fortresses, or palaces, defy time by embodying a profound understanding of materials, engineering, and the symbolic language of architecture.

The Great Wall of China, stretching over 13,000 miles across rugged terrains, remains one of history's most remarkable engineering feats. Constructed over several dynasties, with much of the work occurring during the Ming Dynasty, the wall was originally conceived as a defensive barrier against invading forces. Its construction involved a combination of local materials—stone, tamped earth, wood, and bricks—depending on the region. What makes the Great Wall extraordinary is not simply its length but the way it integrates with the natural topography. Builders adapted the structure to the contours of mountains and valleys, creating a seamless blend of human ingenuity and the natural environment. Watchtowers and fortresses punctuate the wall, serving both as defensive positions and communication points. The wall's continued existence, despite centuries of erosion and human activity, is a testament to the meticulous construction techniques employed and the scale of vision that inspired its creation.

Another marvel that challenges the passage of time is the temple complex at Angkor Wat in Cambodia. Originally constructed in the early 12th century as a Hindu temple dedicated to Vishnu and later converted to a Buddhist site, Angkor Wat is the largest religious monument in the world. Its design reflects a profound understanding of symmetry, proportion, and sacred geometry. The central towers, rising like lotus buds, symbolize Mount Meru, the mythical center of the universe in Hindu cosmology. Builders used sandstone blocks, intricately carved with depictions of deities, mythological scenes, and delicate floral patterns. The precision with which these stones were cut and fitted, without the use of mortar, has allowed the structure to endure through centuries of monsoons, floods, and even periods of neglect. The temple's orientation, aligned with the movements of the sun and stars, further underscores the advanced understanding of astronomy possessed by its creators. Angkor Wat's ability to captivate and inspire awe remains undiminished, drawing millions of visitors each year.

The Colosseum in Rome, constructed in the first century CE during the reign of Emperor Vespasian and completed by his son Titus, stands as a symbol of Roman engineering and architectural brilliance. This massive amphitheater, capable of seating over 50,000 spectators, was designed to host gladiatorial combats, public spectacles, and theatrical performances.

The Colosseum's elliptical shape and tiered seating demonstrate a sophisticated understanding of sightlines and crowd management, ensuring that every spectator had an unobstructed view of the arena. Its construction relied on a combination of concrete, travertine, and volcanic rock, materials chosen for their strength and durability. The system of arches and vaulted corridors not only supported the immense weight of the structure but also allowed for efficient movement of people. Despite earthquakes, looting, and the ravages of time, the Colosseum endures as a monument to the ingenuity of Roman architects and their ability to create spaces that were both functional and monumental.

In the Andes Mountains of Peru, the ancient city of Machu Picchu defies time both physically and symbolically. Built in the 15th century by the Inca emperor Pachacuti, this mountaintop retreat demonstrates a mastery of stone masonry and an intimate relationship with the surrounding environment. The city's structures, including temples, terraces, and residential areas, were constructed without the use of mortar, relying instead on precisely cut stones that fit together so tightly that not even a blade of grass can slide between them. This technique, known as ashlar masonry, allowed Machu Picchu to withstand earthquakes and heavy rainfall, conditions common in the region. The city's layout reflects the Inca's deep spiritual connection to nature, with key structures aligned to astronomical events such as the solstices. Rediscovered in 1911, Machu Picchu remains a powerful reminder of the Inca's architectural and cultural achievements.

The Taj Mahal in Agra, India, is another monumental structure that transcends time, not only for its architectural beauty but also for the story it tells. Built in the 17th century by the Mughal emperor Shah Jahan as a mausoleum for his beloved wife Mumtaz Mahal, the Taj Mahal is a masterpiece of symmetry and craftsmanship. Its white marble façade, inlaid with semi-precious stones forming intricate floral patterns, reflects the Mughal tradition of blending Persian, Indian, and Islamic architectural styles. The central dome, flanked by four minarets, creates a sense of harmony and balance, while the surrounding gardens, laid out in a formal Persian style, symbolize paradise. The Taj Mahal's enduring appeal lies not only in its physical beauty but also in the emotional resonance of its origins. It stands as a monument to love, loss, and the human desire to create something eternal.

Stonehenge, located on the Salisbury Plain in England, is one of the oldest monumental structures that continues to baffle and fascinate. Believed to have been constructed between 3000 and 2000 BCE, this prehistoric stone circle has sparked countless theories regarding its purpose and construction. The arrangement of the massive sarsen stones and smaller bluestones suggests a deep understanding of astronomy, as the site aligns with the solstices and other celestial events. Transporting the stones, some of which weigh up to 25 tons, from quarries located miles away remains a mystery, though it likely involved a combination of sledges, rollers, and human labor. Stonehenge's endurance through millennia of weather and human interference speaks to the ingenuity and determination of its creators.

These monumental structures, each unique in purpose and design, share a common thread: they were built with an understanding of materials, an eye for detail, and a vision that transcended the immediate needs of their time. They remind us of humanity's capacity to dream, innovate, and leave a lasting mark on the world. Their endurance challenges us to consider what we build today and how it might speak to future generations. Through their survival, they continue to connect us to the past, offering lessons in resilience, creativity, and the timeless pursuit of excellence.

CHAPTER 3: ANCIENT MACHINES AND MECHANISMS

The Antikythera Mechanism: The World's First Computer

Discovered in 1901 among the remains of a Roman-era shipwreck off the coast of the Greek island of Antikythera, the Antikythera Mechanism is one of the most extraordinary artifacts of ancient engineering. This intricate device, dated to around 150–100 BCE, has reshaped our understanding of the technological capabilities of ancient civilizations. Often described as the world's first analog computer, the mechanism was designed to track celestial movements and predict astronomical events with astonishing precision. Its complexity, unmatched for over a millennium, reveals a level of scientific and mechanical sophistication that few would have attributed to the ancient Greeks before its discovery.

The Antikythera Mechanism, at first glance, appeared to be little more than a collection of corroded bronze fragments. It took decades of study and technological advancements to uncover the true nature of the device. X-ray imaging and 3D scanning eventually revealed a system of interlocking gears, dials, and inscriptions. These components were housed in a wooden box roughly the size of a shoebox, and their arrangement suggested a highly specialized function. The sheer density of the gears—over 30 of them, some with as many as 223 teeth—immediately suggested a purpose far beyond simple timekeeping or navigation.

The primary function of the mechanism was astronomical. It could predict the positions of the sun, moon, and planets, as well as track the phases of the moon and forecast eclipses. One of its dials represented the zodiac, divided into 12 sections corresponding to the constellations, while another displayed the Egyptian calendar, which was widely used in ancient Greece. The mechanism's ability to synchronize these different systems of time and space speaks to both its mechanical ingenuity and the depth of astronomical knowledge possessed by its creators. The Greeks had long studied the heavens, but the Antikythera Mechanism translated that theoretical knowledge into a practical, physical tool.

One of the most remarkable aspects of the mechanism is its ability to account for the irregularities in the moon's orbit. The moon's motion is not perfectly circular but elliptical, and its speed varies as it moves closer to or farther from the Earth. The designers of the Antikythera Mechanism incorporated a pin-and-slot mechanism to replicate this variability—a feature that would not reappear in European clockmaking until the 14th century. This innovation demonstrates not only a keen understanding of celestial mechanics but also an extraordinary ability to translate that understanding into a functional mechanical system.

The predictive capabilities of the mechanism extended to eclipses, which were of great importance in ancient times for both practical and religious reasons. The device could forecast lunar and solar eclipses by using a dial that tracked the 223-month Saros cycle, the period after which eclipses repeat in a predictable pattern. By turning a crank, the user could simulate the passage of time and observe when eclipses would occur. Inscriptions on the device even indicated the color of future eclipses, which the Greeks believed could carry significant omens. This ability to predict such events with accuracy would have been invaluable for planning agricultural, religious, and political activities.

The Antikythera Mechanism's craftsmanship also speaks volumes about the technological infrastructure of the period. The precision with which the gears were cut and assembled suggests the use of advanced tools and techniques. Bronze, the primary material, was carefully shaped and polished, indicating a high level of metallurgical skill. While the exact workshop or inventor remains unknown, historical records hint at possible connections to renowned figures such as Hipparchus, a Greek astronomer and mathematician whose work on celestial phenomena aligns closely with the functions of the mechanism. Whether or not he directly contributed to its creation, the device reflects the intellectual atmosphere of Hellenistic Greece, a period marked by intense scientific curiosity and innovation.

The mystery of how such a sophisticated device was lost to history for centuries remains a compelling question. The decline of the Hellenistic world, followed by the dominance of Rome and the eventual fall of the Roman Empire, likely contributed to the disappearance of the knowledge and techniques required to produce such mechanisms. The Antikythera Mechanism was not merely an isolated marvel but part of a broader tradition of Greek engineering and science that was disrupted by political and social upheaval. Its rediscovery has forced historians to reconsider the narrative of technological progress, challenging the assumption that complex machines are solely the product of the modern age.

The mechanism's shipwreck context offers further insights into its significance. The vessel carrying it was likely transporting luxury goods from the eastern Mediterranean to Rome, suggesting that the device may have been commissioned for a wealthy patron or scholar. Its portability implies it could have been used as a teaching tool or a personal instrument for tracking celestial events. Whatever its intended role, the Antikythera Mechanism underscores the interconnectedness of ancient societies, where ideas and innovations could travel alongside goods and people.

Modern efforts to replicate the mechanism have deepened our appreciation for its complexity. Engineers and scholars have created working models based on the surviving fragments, demonstrating how the various gears and dials operated in concert. These reconstructions not only confirm the mechanism's functions but also highlight the level of precision required to build it. Every gear, tooth, and inscription had to be crafted with exacting accuracy, a task that demanded both technical skill and a profound understanding of astronomy.

The Antikythera Mechanism is not merely a relic of the past; it is a bridge between ancient ingenuity and modern science. Its discovery has inspired new investigations into the technological capabilities of ancient civilizations, revealing a legacy of innovation that continues to shape our understanding of history. The device serves as a reminder that the pursuit of knowledge is a timeless endeavor, driven by the same curiosity and creativity that define humanity across all ages. Its gears, long silent and corroded, still turn in the minds of those who seek to uncover the secrets of the past and apply them to the challenges of the present.

Hydraulic Engineering in Early Civilizations

Water has always been a vital resource for human survival and development, and the civilizations of antiquity understood this with remarkable clarity. From the rivers of Mesopotamia to the arid landscapes of the Andes, hydraulic engineering emerged as a cornerstone of societal advancement. Early civilizations devised innovative systems for irrigation, flood control, water storage, and urban supply, demonstrating a profound comprehension of natural forces and resource management. These systems not only supported agriculture and sustained growing populations but also reflected the social, political, and spiritual priorities of their builders. The ingenuity of these early hydraulic engineers laid the groundwork for many of the practices still in use today.

In the fertile crescent of Mesopotamia, the Sumerians were among the first to harness water for large-scale agriculture. Situated between the Tigris and Euphrates rivers, their land was both a gift and a challenge. The rivers provided abundant water, but their unpredictable flooding posed a constant threat to crops and settlements. To address this, the Sumerians constructed an intricate network of canals, levees, and reservoirs. These canals diverted water from the rivers to irrigate fields, enabling year-round farming in a region where rainfall was scarce. The levees helped to control flooding, protecting both crops and infrastructure. The scale and organization required to maintain these systems highlight the central role of water management in Sumerian society. It required coordinated labor, advanced planning, and the oversight of a centralized authority, often tied to temple institutions that governed both spiritual and practical life.

Farther to the west, the ancient Egyptians developed their own sophisticated hydraulic systems along the Nile River. The Nile's annual inundation was the lifeblood of Egyptian agriculture, depositing nutrient-rich silt on the floodplains. Rather than attempting to control the river as the Sumerians did, the Egyptians embraced its natural rhythms. They constructed basins and dikes to capture and store floodwaters, gradually releasing them to irrigate surrounding fields. These systems allowed farmers to cultivate crops such as wheat and barley with remarkable efficiency. The organization of labor to build and maintain these systems was closely tied to the centralized power of the pharaoh, whose authority was seen as essential to ensuring the prosperity of the land. Hydraulic engineering thus became not only a practical necessity but also a means of reinforcing political and religious order.

The Indus Valley Civilization, centered in what is now Pakistan and northwest India, pushed the boundaries of hydraulic engineering to an extraordinary degree. Cities like Mohenjo-Daro and Harappa featured advanced drainage systems, with covered sewers running beneath the streets to channel wastewater away from residential areas. Wells were common, providing reliable access to clean water for drinking and bathing. These features suggest a highly organized society that prioritized hygiene and public health. The presence of large, centrally located water tanks, such as the Great Bath of Mohenjo-Daro, indicates that water was not only a practical resource but also held cultural and possibly religious significance. The uniformity of these systems across multiple cities points to a shared architectural and engineering knowledge, coordinated on a scale that remains impressive even by modern standards.

In the arid landscapes of ancient Persia, the invention of qanats revolutionized water management. Qanats are underground channels that transport water from aquifers in the mountains to settlements and agricultural fields in the valleys below. This system, developed as early as the first millennium BCE, relied on a series of vertical shafts dug into the ground, connected by a gently sloping tunnel that allowed gravity to carry water over long distances. The genius of the qanat lies in its ability to minimize water loss through evaporation, a critical advantage in the hot, dry climate of Persia. These systems not only sustained agriculture but also supported the growth of cities and trade networks, playing a crucial role in the expansion of the Persian Empire. The principles of qanat construction spread far and wide, influencing water management practices in regions as distant as North Africa and Spain.

In the Americas, the Inca civilization demonstrated remarkable hydraulic ingenuity in the Andes Mountains. Faced with steep, rugged terrain and unpredictable rainfall, the Incas developed terraced farming systems that integrated water management into their very design. Stone-lined channels and aqueducts carried water from mountain springs to the terraces, ensuring a steady supply for crops such as maize and potatoes. These terraces reduced soil erosion, conserved water, and maximized arable land in a challenging environment. At the heart of the Inca Empire, the city of Cusco featured an elaborate system of canals and fountains that distributed water throughout the urban center. Machu Picchu, the famous mountaintop retreat, exemplifies the Incas' mastery of hydraulic engineering, with its carefully designed drainage systems and water channels that continue to function centuries after their construction.

The Romans elevated hydraulic engineering to an unprecedented level of sophistication and scale. Their aqueducts, which carried water from distant sources to cities and towns, stand as iconic symbols of Roman engineering prowess. These structures, built with a combination of stone, concrete, and arches, relied on precise gradients to maintain a steady flow of water over vast distances. The aqueducts supplied public baths, fountains, and private homes, ensuring that water was accessible to all levels of society. The Cloaca Maxima, one of the world's earliest sewer systems, drained wastewater from the city of Rome into the Tiber River, reducing the risk of disease and maintaining sanitation. Roman engineers also developed techniques for dam construction, enabling the storage and regulation of water supplies. These innovations supported the expansion of the empire, providing the infrastructure necessary for urban growth and economic prosperity.

The ingenuity of hydraulic engineering in early civilizations was not limited to large-scale systems. Many societies developed localized techniques tailored to their specific environments. The ancient Chinese, for example, constructed extensive irrigation systems to support rice cultivation, while also building dikes and levees to manage the mighty Yellow River. In Southeast Asia, the Khmer Empire created vast reservoirs and canals at Angkor, enabling the cultivation of rice on a monumental scale and sustaining one of the largest pre-industrial urban centers in history. Each of these systems reflects a deep understanding of the interplay between water, land, and human activity.

The achievements of early hydraulic engineers continue to inspire awe and admiration. These systems were more than mere technical feats; they were expressions of a society's values, priorities, and understanding of the natural world. By harnessing the power of water, ancient civilizations not only sustained themselves but also laid the foundations for many of the principles and practices that we rely on today. Their legacy endures, reminding us of the profound connection between human ingenuity and the forces of nature.

The Ingenious Simplicity of the Archimedes Screw

The Archimedes screw, a deceptively simple yet profoundly effective piece of ancient engineering, has stood the test of time as a symbol of human ingenuity. Attributed to the Greek mathematician and inventor Archimedes of Syracuse in the 3rd century BCE, the device was originally conceived to move water efficiently from lower elevations to higher ones. Its simplicity belies its significance; the Archimedes screw is not only a marvel of mechanical design but also a cornerstone of hydraulic technology, with applications that have resonated through centuries and across continents.

The design of the Archimedes screw is as elegant as it is logical. It consists of a helical screw encased within a hollow cylinder or open trough. When the device is angled appropriately and rotated, it lifts water or other materials from one level to another with minimal effort. The mechanism's operation relies on basic physical principles—gravity, buoyancy, and rotational motion—making it an intuitive and efficient solution for a wide range of practical challenges. While Archimedes is credited with its invention, variations of the screw mechanism may have existed earlier in Mesopotamia and Egypt, suggesting that the concept was a culmination of ancient engineering knowledge, refined and perfected under his guidance.

The primary application of the Archimedes screw in antiquity was irrigation, a critical necessity in agrarian societies. In ancient Egypt, where it is believed the screw may have been introduced after Archimedes' time, it proved invaluable for lifting water from the Nile River to irrigate fields on higher ground. Farmers could use the device to transport water across terraces, sustaining crops even during dry seasons. Its ability to function with minimal labor and maintenance made it accessible to communities with limited resources. The screw's design, often constructed from wood and reinforced with bronze or copper fittings, allowed it to withstand prolonged exposure to water while remaining lightweight enough to be portable.

Beyond irrigation, the Archimedes screw found utility in a variety of other contexts. In ancient Greece and Rome, it was employed in drainage systems to remove water from flooded mines or marshlands. The Romans, known for their engineering prowess, incorporated the screw into more complex systems, such as aqueduct maintenance and the operation of public baths. By controlling the flow and elevation of water, the device allowed for the efficient management of urban water supplies, contributing to the health and sanitation of growing cities. Its versatility extended to industrial applications as well, where it was used to transport materials like grain, sand, and even wine in certain cases. The adaptability of the Archimedes screw underscores its enduring relevance, as the same basic principles remain in use today.

The mechanics of the Archimedes screw are remarkably straightforward. As the screw rotates, pockets of water (or other materials) are trapped between the threads of the helix and the inner surface of the cylinder. These pockets are carried upward as the rotation continues, effectively defying gravity without the need for complex machinery. The angle of the screw and the speed of rotation determine its efficiency, with steeper angles requiring more energy but lifting water to greater heights. This simplicity is its genius; the device can be powered manually, by animals, or even by windmills, depending on the available resources and specific needs of the user. Its versatility in energy sources further enhanced its appeal across different regions and eras.

The influence of the Archimedes screw extended far beyond the ancient Mediterranean world. Its design spread through trade, conquest, and cultural exchange, finding applications in regions as diverse as India, China, and the Middle East. In medieval Europe, the screw was adapted for use in watermills and other early industrial processes. The Renaissance saw a resurgence in interest in classical technologies, and the Archimedes screw was studied, modified, and incorporated into new mechanical systems. By the 18th and 19th centuries, it had become a staple in flood control projects, particularly in the Netherlands, where it was instrumental in draining polders and reclaiming land from the sea. The Dutch adaptation of the screw, often powered by windmills, stands as a testament to its enduring utility and adaptability.

Modern engineering has not rendered the Archimedes screw obsolete; on the contrary, it remains a vital component in numerous industries. In wastewater treatment plants, the device is used to transport sludge and other materials with minimal risk of clogging. Its ability to handle varying volumes and densities makes it ideal for such applications. In hydropower generation, the reverse operation of the Archimedes screw—allowing water to flow downward through the device—has been harnessed to produce electricity. This environmentally friendly technology, known as the Archimedean screw turbine, demonstrates the timelessness of the original design. Even today, the screw's principles are applied in everything from agricultural irrigation systems to food processing equipment.

The enduring legacy of the Archimedes screw lies in its ingenious combination of simplicity and effectiveness. It exemplifies how a deep understanding of natural forces, combined with a practical mindset, can yield solutions that transcend time and cultural boundaries. Archimedes himself, renowned for his contributions to mathematics, physics, and engineering, likely viewed the screw as just one of many tools in his intellectual arsenal. Yet its impact has been profound, shaping the development of civilizations and influencing countless technological advancements.

The story of the Archimedes screw is one of innovation born from necessity, a reminder of humanity's ability to adapt and thrive in the face of challenges. Its presence in ancient fields, bustling Roman cities, and modern industrial facilities speaks to its universal appeal and practicality. By bridging the gap between ancient ingenuity and contemporary technology, the Archimedes screw continues to inspire engineers, historians, and inventors alike. It stands as a testament to the enduring power of simple ideas, proving that the most effective solutions are often those that work in harmony with the fundamental laws of nature.

Chapter 4: Communication Across Time

Early Writing Systems: From Cuneiform to Alphabets

The emergence of writing systems was one of the most transformative developments in human history, enabling the preservation of knowledge, the administration of complex societies, and the expression of culture and thought across generations. Before writing, oral traditions were the primary means of communication and record-keeping. While effective in smaller, close-knit groups, oral transmission was inherently fragile, vulnerable to loss and distortion over time. The invention of writing offered a solution, allowing information to transcend the limitations of memory and geography. From the earliest wedge-shaped impressions of cuneiform to the fluid, adaptable alphabets that would dominate later civilizations, the evolution of writing systems tells the story of humanity's quest to make thought permanent.

The earliest known writing system, cuneiform, emerged in Mesopotamia around 3100 BCE, developed by the Sumerians. This system began as a method for recording economic transactions, such as the distribution of grain or the allocation of livestock. Using a stylus made from reeds, scribes pressed wedge-shaped marks into clay tablets, creating a script that was both practical and durable. The symbol-based system initially consisted of pictograms, which represented objects or concepts directly. Over time, these pictograms became increasingly abstract, evolving into a combination of logograms (symbols representing words or ideas) and phonetic elements. This progression allowed cuneiform to expand beyond economic contexts, encompassing legal codes, literature, and scientific texts. The Epic of Gilgamesh, one of the oldest known works of literature, was etched in cuneiform, illustrating how the system evolved to articulate complex narratives and human emotions.

Cuneiform's influence extended well beyond the Sumerians. The Akkadians, Babylonians, Assyrians, and other Mesopotamian cultures adopted and adapted the system for their own languages. Mastery of cuneiform became a specialized skill, often confined to an educated elite of scribes who underwent rigorous training. These scribes wielded significant power, as their ability to record and interpret information was essential to the functioning of government, trade, and religion. The durability of clay tablets contributed to the survival of thousands of cuneiform texts, offering modern scholars a window into the daily lives, beliefs, and governance of ancient Mesopotamian societies.

Parallel to Mesopotamia, the ancient Egyptians developed their own writing system: hieroglyphics. Emerging around 3100 BCE, hieroglyphs combined pictorial and phonetic elements, creating a visually striking script that adorned temple walls, tombs, and monuments. Unlike cuneiform, which prioritized practicality, hieroglyphics often served ceremonial and religious purposes. The intricate carvings were believed to hold divine power, ensuring the deceased's safe passage to the afterlife or commemorating the achievements of pharaohs and gods. For more mundane uses, the Egyptians employed hieratic, a cursive script written on papyrus, which allowed for faster and more practical record-keeping. The coexistence of these scripts reflects the dynamic relationship between art, religion, and administration in ancient Egypt.

The Phoenicians, a seafaring people who flourished around 1500 BCE along the eastern Mediterranean coast, revolutionized writing by simplifying it into an alphabetic system. Unlike cuneiform and hieroglyphics, which required hundreds or even thousands of symbols, the Phoenician alphabet relied on a small set of symbols to represent individual sounds. This phonetic approach made writing more accessible and versatile, as it could be adapted to different languages with relative ease. The Phoenician alphabet spread rapidly through trade, laying the foundation for Greek, Latin, and other later alphabets. Its simplicity marked a turning point in the history of writing, democratizing literacy and enabling broader participation in written communication.

The Greeks adopted the Phoenician alphabet around the 8th century BCE, modifying it to include vowels, a feature absent from the original. This innovation enhanced the system's expressiveness, making it suitable for recording complex ideas and literary works. Greek writers used the alphabet to compose epic poetry, philosophy, and scientific treatises, leaving a legacy that continues to shape Western thought. The flexibility of the Greek alphabet allowed it to evolve further, influencing the development of the Latin alphabet used in much of the modern world.

In parallel, the ancient Indian subcontinent saw the rise of its own writing systems, such as Brahmi, which emerged around the 3rd century BCE. Brahmi served as the precursor to many of the scripts used in South Asia today, including Devanagari, the script of Sanskrit and Hindi. Like the Phoenician alphabet, Brahmi was phonetic, but it also incorporated diacritical marks to represent variations in sound, reflecting the linguistic diversity of the region. The inscriptions of Emperor Ashoka, carved into stone pillars and rock faces, are among the earliest surviving examples of Brahmi, offering insights into the spread of Buddhism and the administration of the Mauryan Empire.

In East Asia, the Chinese developed their own logographic writing system, which remains in use today. Chinese characters, each representing a word or concept, originated as pictograms carved into oracle bones during the Shang Dynasty (c. 1200 BCE). Over time, these characters became more abstract, evolving into a highly sophisticated system capable of conveying subtle meanings and nuances. Unlike alphabetic systems, Chinese writing does not rely on phonetics, which has contributed to its continuity across millennia despite changes in spoken language. The enduring nature of Chinese characters underscores their adaptability and cultural significance.

The evolution of writing systems was not a linear process but a mosaic of innovation, adaptation, and cultural exchange. The hieroglyphs of Egypt influenced the development of the Proto-Sinaitic script, which in turn gave rise to the Phoenician alphabet. The spread of alphabetic writing through trade and conquest demonstrates how interconnected ancient civilizations were, exchanging not only goods but also ideas. Writing systems adapted to the needs and contexts of their users, from the monumental inscriptions of kings to the everyday transactions of merchants.

The invention of writing transformed human history by enabling the preservation and transmission of knowledge across time and space. It allowed societies to organize themselves more effectively, codify laws, and express their beliefs and values. Writing systems also became symbols of identity and power, reflecting the priorities and achievements of the cultures that created them. From the clay tablets of Mesopotamia to the parchment scrolls of medieval Europe, the legacy of early writing systems continues to shape the way we communicate, remember, and imagine. The marks left by ancient scribes endure not only as records of the past but as reminders of the enduring human desire to connect and create.

The Art of Memory and Oral Traditions

Long before the invention of writing systems, memory served as the cornerstone of human communication, knowledge preservation, and cultural continuity. Oral traditions, transmitted from one generation to the next, carried the weight of collective wisdom, history, and identity. These traditions were not merely functional; they were deeply artistic, woven into stories, songs, and rituals that engaged the mind and fostered communal bonds. The art of memory, honed over millennia, was a sophisticated skill that allowed societies to thrive without the need for written records. By understanding how oral cultures preserved their knowledge, we gain insight into the ingenuity and creativity that shaped early human communication.

In societies that relied solely on oral transmission, memory was not an individual endeavor but a communal responsibility. Elders, storytellers, priests, and other designated custodians of knowledge played vital roles as living repositories of cultural heritage. These individuals often underwent rigorous training to master their craft, developing mnemonic techniques that allowed them to recall vast amounts of information with remarkable accuracy. Repetition, rhythm, and rhyme were essential tools in this process. By embedding information within songs, chants, or poetic structures, speakers could make it both memorable and engaging. This fusion of function and artistry elevated oral traditions beyond simple record-keeping, transforming them into a dynamic and participatory experience.

The power of storytelling was central to oral traditions, as narratives provided a framework for organizing and transmitting knowledge. Stories allowed abstract concepts, historical events, and moral lessons to take on concrete and relatable forms. Myths and legends, often populated by gods, heroes, and archetypal figures, served as vehicles for explaining natural phenomena, social norms, and the origins of the world. In many cases, these stories were not fixed but evolved over time, adapting to the needs and contexts of their audiences. This adaptability ensured their relevance and longevity, even as the societies that created them underwent change.

Oral traditions often relied on specific mnemonic devices to aid memory. One of the most enduring techniques was the use of formulaic expressions, such as epithets, repeated phrases, or stock descriptions. These elements acted as cues, helping storytellers navigate complex narratives while maintaining consistency. The Homeric epics, for example, are filled with phrases like "swift-footed Achilles" or "rosy-fingered dawn," which not only enhance the poetic quality of the text but also serve as memory aids. Similarly, genealogies, proverbs, and aphorisms were structured in ways that made them easier to recall. By organizing information into patterns or sequences, oral cultures ensured its retention across generations.

In addition to verbal techniques, oral traditions often incorporated visual and spatial elements to reinforce memory. Storytellers and speakers might use gestures, facial expressions, or props to bring their narratives to life. In some cultures, memory was tied to specific locations or physical objects. The Aboriginal peoples of Australia, for instance, used "songlines" to encode knowledge about their environment, embedding information about landmarks, resources, and routes into songs that could be "read" as they traveled across the land. This integration of memory with place created a vivid and immersive way of preserving and transmitting knowledge.

Rituals and ceremonies also played a crucial role in oral traditions, providing structured settings in which knowledge could be performed and reinforced. These events often combined storytelling, music, dance, and symbolic actions, creating a multisensory experience that engaged participants on multiple levels. By embedding information within rituals, oral cultures ensured its ongoing transmission, as the act of performing the ritual became inseparable from the knowledge it contained. Religious ceremonies, initiation rites, and seasonal festivals all served as opportunities to pass down history, values, and practical knowledge while strengthening social cohesion.

The transition from orality to literacy brought profound changes to the way societies preserved and transmitted knowledge, yet oral traditions did not disappear. Instead, they adapted, coexisting with written records and influencing the development of new forms of communication. In many cultures, oral and written traditions became mutually reinforcing, with each serving distinct but complementary purposes. For example, early written texts often retained the rhythms, repetitions, and structures of oral speech, reflecting their origins in oral performance. Even today, oral traditions remain vibrant in communities around the world, demonstrating their resilience and adaptability.

The art of memory, as practiced in oral cultures, reveals a deep understanding of the human mind and its capacity for creativity. By embedding knowledge in stories, songs, and rituals, oral traditions transformed memory into a collective and participatory process. They connected individuals to their communities, their histories, and the world around them, fostering a sense of continuity and belonging. In an age dominated by written and digital forms of communication, the lessons of oral traditions remain relevant, reminding us of the power of storytelling and the enduring value of human connection.

Signal Towers, Smoke, and Early Long-Distance Communication

Across the vast stretches of human history, the need to communicate over long distances has driven extraordinary ingenuity. Long before the advent of written messages or electronic signals, civilizations devised systems that could relay vital information swiftly, transcending geographical barriers. Signal towers, smoke signals, and other forms of early long-distance communication reveal the resourcefulness of ancient societies as they grappled with the challenges of delivering urgent messages in an era devoid of modern technology. These methods served as lifelines for military strategies, governance, and community coordination, laying the groundwork for the communication networks that would follow in later centuries.

Signal towers, constructed across landscapes to form relay systems, were among the most effective methods for transmitting messages over long distances in ancient times. The Achaemenid Empire of Persia, which spanned vast territories from the Mediterranean to the Indus Valley, relied on an intricate network of watchtowers for military and administrative communication. Positioned at regular intervals, these towers were staffed with guards who kept a vigilant watch for incoming signals. Messages were conveyed using fire or reflective surfaces, often at night when the flames of a beacon could be seen from miles away. This system allowed the Persian kings to relay commands and receive reports from their provinces in astonishingly short periods, given the limitations of the era. The speed and reliability of the network played a critical role in maintaining control over such a sprawling empire.

The Greeks and Romans also embraced the concept of signal towers, adapting them to their specific needs. During the Peloponnesian War, for instance, the Greeks used fire signals to warn of enemy movements or coordinate naval operations. The historian Polybius later refined the system by introducing a method to encode messages using torches, enabling the transmission of more complex information than simple alerts. The Romans, famed for their organizational prowess, incorporated signal towers into their military infrastructure, constructing them along roads and borders to relay information to and from their legions. The Roman system, integrated with their extensive road network, provided a level of communication efficiency that contributed significantly to the empire's stability and expansion.

Smoke signals, another ancient method of long-distance communication, were particularly well-suited to nomadic and semi-nomadic societies. The indigenous peoples of North America, including the Plains tribes, used smoke to send messages across vast open landscapes. By varying the number, size, and frequency of smoke puffs, they could encode specific messages, often related to hunting, danger, or the movement of rival groups. The simplicity and adaptability of smoke signals made them invaluable in environments where other forms of communication were impractical. Similarly, in ancient China, smoke signals formed a critical component of the Great Wall's defensive system. Beacon towers along the wall could transmit warnings of an approaching enemy in mere hours, covering hundreds of miles and enabling swift military responses.

In Africa, the use of drum signals provided another ingenious solution to the challenges of long-distance communication. Drums, with their resonant tones, could carry messages across dense forests and open savannas, reaching distances that would have taken days to traverse on foot. By manipulating the rhythm, pitch, and tempo of the drumming, skilled operators could encode complex messages that were understood by distant communities. This system, known as "talking drums," was particularly prevalent in West Africa, where it served not only practical purposes but also cultural and ceremonial roles. The linguistic richness of many African languages, with their reliance on tonal variations, made them uniquely suited to this form of communication.

Each of these methods, though simple by contemporary standards, relied on a profound understanding of the natural world. The placement of signal towers took into account topography, ensuring that messages could travel unobstructed across valleys and mountains. Smoke signals required careful attention to wind patterns and fuel selection, as the type of material burned influenced the color, density, and visibility of the smoke. Drum signals exploited the acoustic properties of the environment, with operators positioning themselves to maximize the resonance and reach of their messages. These early systems reveal a remarkable ability to adapt to environmental constraints, turning natural elements into tools of communication.

The limitations of these methods, however, were as apparent as their advantages. Weather conditions, such as fog, rain, or high winds, could disrupt the visibility of fire and smoke signals or dampen the sound of drums. The reliance on human operators introduced the possibility of error or delay, particularly over extended networks. Encoding and decoding messages required a shared understanding of the system, which limited its use to specific groups or communities. Despite these challenges, the effectiveness of these communication systems in their respective contexts cannot be overstated. They provided a means to convey information quickly and efficiently, often making the difference between success and failure in critical situations.

The legacy of early long-distance communication methods is evident in the systems that followed. The principles underlying signal towers and smoke signals—relay networks, encoded messages, and the use of natural elements—can be seen in the development of semaphore lines, telegraphs, and even modern digital communication. These early innovations demonstrated the importance of speed, accuracy, and redundancy in communication, principles that remain central to the field today. Moreover, they highlight the universal human drive to connect and coordinate, a drive that transcends time, culture, and technology.

The ingenuity of these systems lies not only in their technical aspects but also in the human stories they represent. The guard lighting a beacon on a lonely mountaintop, the scout sending smoke signals across a windswept plain, the drummer relaying a message through the dense forest—all were participants in a shared endeavor to bridge the distances that separated them. Their efforts, though often overlooked in the grand narratives of history, underscore the resilience and creativity of the human spirit in the face of isolation and challenge. These early methods of communication, born of necessity and shaped by resourcefulness, remind us of the enduring quest to transcend barriers and connect with one another.

The Influence of Ancient Maps on Modern Cartography

Maps are not merely tools of navigation; they are reflections of the worldviews, knowledge, and ambitions of the societies that create them. Ancient cartography, born from necessity and curiosity, laid the foundational principles that continue to shape modern mapmaking. These early maps were more than geographical representations; they were expressions of power, trade, culture, and connection. From the clay tablets of Mesopotamia to the detailed charts of the Greco-Roman world, the influence of ancient maps on modern cartography is profound, revealing a lineage of innovation and adaptation that has persisted across millennia.

One of the earliest known maps, carved into a clay tablet in the city of Nippur around 1500 BCE, offers a glimpse into the Mesopotamian understanding of the world. Rather than striving for geographical accuracy as modern maps do, this map was symbolic, depicting a world centered on the Euphrates River and surrounded by mythical lands. Its purpose was not to guide travelers but to convey a cosmological vision, anchoring Mesopotamian society within a divine framework. Such maps served as more than practical tools; they were instruments of knowledge and identity, shaping how people perceived their place in the universe.

In ancient Egypt, cartography found its roots in the management of resources and the organization of society. The annual flooding of the Nile required precise measurements and delineations of land for agricultural purposes. Surveyors, known as "rope stretchers," used early forms of geometric mapping to restore boundaries after the inundation. The Turin Papyrus Map, dating to around 1150 BCE, is among the oldest surviving topographical maps. Created to document mining expeditions, it includes details of roads, mountains, and gold deposits, demonstrating a practical application of cartography that extended beyond agriculture. The Egyptians' focus on utility influenced later mapmaking traditions, emphasizing functionality alongside representation.

The Greeks revolutionized cartography by introducing a scientific approach to understanding the world. Pioneers like Anaximander and Hecataeus of Miletus sought to map the Earth based on empirical observations rather than mythological interpretations. Anaximander's map, created in the 6th century BCE, depicted the known world as a circular disk surrounded by ocean, reflecting the limited geographical knowledge of the time. Though rudimentary, it marked a departure from symbolic maps, laying the groundwork for more systematic explorations. Hecataeus built on this foundation, compiling a detailed account of lands and peoples in his "Ges Periodos," an early attempt at documenting the breadth of human civilization through cartographic means.

The work of Claudius Ptolemy in the 2nd century CE represents one of the most significant milestones in ancient cartography. His treatise, "Geographia," synthesized earlier Greek and Roman knowledge, introducing concepts that would shape mapmaking for centuries. Ptolemy devised a coordinate system based on latitude and longitude, allowing for the precise placement of locations on a grid. He also emphasized the importance of mathematical calculations in creating accurate maps, a principle that underpins modern cartography. While many of Ptolemy's maps contained inaccuracies—such as the exaggerated size of Asia—they demonstrated an ambition to depict the entire known world in a systematic, coherent manner.

The Roman Empire, with its vast territorial expanse, relied on maps for administrative and military purposes. The "Tabula Peutingeriana," a 4th-century CE Roman road map, illustrates the empire's network of roads, cities, and landmarks. Unlike Ptolemaic maps, it was not designed for geographic accuracy but rather for practical use, enabling travelers to navigate the empire's infrastructure. Its linear, schematic style highlights the Roman emphasis on connectivity and control, reflecting the utilitarian aspects of cartography that remain relevant in transportation and urban planning today.

Ancient Chinese cartography developed independently, following its own trajectory of innovation. Early Chinese maps, such as those from the Han Dynasty, combined geographical features with administrative boundaries, emphasizing the integration of natural and political landscapes. The 3rd-century mapmaker Pei Xiu introduced principles that anticipated modern cartographic techniques, including the use of scales and grids. His work demonstrated a meticulous attention to detail, capturing the complexity of the Chinese Empire's terrain and governance. These maps influenced East Asian cartography for centuries, showcasing an alternative tradition of mapmaking that paralleled developments in the West.

The Islamic Golden Age saw a synthesis of Greek, Roman, Persian, and Indian cartographic knowledge, culminating in the creation of maps that were both scientifically advanced and artistically intricate. Al-Idrisi's 12th-century world map, commissioned by the Norman king Roger II of Sicily, exemplifies this fusion. Al-Idrisi combined Ptolemaic principles with firsthand accounts from travelers, producing a map that was remarkably accurate for its time. His work, along with that of other Islamic scholars, preserved and expanded upon ancient traditions, bridging the gap between antiquity and the Renaissance.

The influence of ancient maps on modern cartography is evident in the persistence of key principles. The use of coordinate systems, first articulated by Ptolemy, remains central to contemporary mapping technologies, from paper atlases to GPS. The emphasis on functionality, seen in Egyptian land surveys and Roman road maps, continues to inform practical applications such as urban planning and navigation. Even the artistic elements of ancient maps, with their intricate designs and symbolic representations, find echoes in the aesthetic considerations of modern cartographic design.

Beyond their technical contributions, ancient maps remind us of the evolving relationship between humanity and its environment. They reflect not only the geographical knowledge of their creators but also their cultural values, priorities, and aspirations. As modern cartographers strive for ever-greater precision and comprehensiveness, the legacy of ancient maps serves as a reminder that cartography is as much an art as it is a science. It is a dialogue between the known and the unknown, a testament to the enduring human desire to explore, understand, and represent the world.

Preserving Knowledge: Libraries of the Ancient World

The libraries of the ancient world were more than mere repositories of texts; they were the epicenters of intellectual life, the guardians of knowledge, and the symbols of human ambition to understand and preserve the vast complexities of existence. Built by rulers, scholars, and civilizations determined to preserve their heritage and expand their understanding of the world, these libraries stood as monuments to the power of ideas. While the modern world takes the accessibility of information for granted, the creation and maintenance of ancient libraries required extraordinary effort and vision. They were fragile treasures, dependent on the labor of scribes, the foresight of leaders, and the peace of empires. Despite their vulnerability to war, neglect, and time, the influence of these early institutions continues to resonate in the way knowledge is curated and disseminated today.

Among the most legendary of these institutions was the Great Library of Alexandria, a beacon of learning in the ancient Mediterranean. Founded in the early 3rd century BCE by Ptolemy I or his son Ptolemy II, it was intended to gather all the knowledge of the known world under one roof. Situated in the vibrant city of Alexandria, a cultural crossroads of Greek, Egyptian, and other influences, the library became a magnet for scholars, scientists, and philosophers. Its collection, said to number hundreds of thousands of scrolls, was painstakingly acquired through an ambitious and sometimes controversial process. Ships arriving in Alexandria were searched for texts, which were copied by scribes before the originals were sometimes kept. The library's mission was not merely to store knowledge but to synthesize and produce it, fostering groundbreaking work in mathematics, astronomy, medicine, and literature. Figures such as Euclid, Archimedes, and Eratosthenes either studied there or were influenced by its resources, cementing Alexandria's role as the intellectual heart of the ancient world. The tragic loss of the library, through a series of events spanning centuries, remains one of history's great cultural catastrophes, a reminder of the fragility of knowledge when it depends on physical media.

Further east, the libraries of Mesopotamia represent some of the earliest and most enduring examples of humanity's dedication to preserving knowledge. The Library of Ashurbanipal in Nineveh, established in the 7th century BCE by the Assyrian king Ashurbanipal, stands out as a testament to this tradition. Unlike the scrolls of Alexandria, the texts in Ashurbanipal's library were inscribed on clay tablets in cuneiform script, a medium far more durable than papyrus. The collection included thousands of works on topics ranging from astronomy and medicine to mythology and law, with the Epic of Gilgamesh being one of its most famous treasures. Ashurbanipal himself was a scholar-king, fluent in multiple languages, and his efforts to preserve and expand his library reflected a personal commitment to knowledge. The library's discovery in the 19th century revealed the sophistication of ancient Mesopotamian scholarship, offering modern researchers invaluable insights into the early civilizations that shaped human history.

In ancient Egypt, temple libraries served as centers of learning and religious authority. These collections, often overseen by priests, contained texts on theology, astronomy, medicine, and rituals, written in hieroglyphs or hieratic script on papyrus scrolls. The House of Life, a term used to describe temple scriptoriums and libraries, was not only a repository of texts but also a place where knowledge was actively created and transmitted. These institutions were deeply intertwined with the spiritual and administrative life of Egypt, reflecting a view of knowledge as sacred and integral to the cosmic order. The texts preserved in these libraries influenced later cultures, particularly through their transmission to the Greek and Roman worlds.

In the Indian subcontinent, the ancient libraries attached to Buddhist monasteries became hubs of intellectual and spiritual activity. Institutions like Nalanda, which flourished from the 5th to the 12th centuries CE, housed vast collections of manuscripts on philosophy, medicine, mathematics, and the arts. Nalanda was more than a library—it was an entire university, attracting scholars from as far as China, Korea, and Central Asia. The texts preserved and studied there played a crucial role in the development of Buddhist thought and its dissemination across Asia. The destruction of Nalanda by invading forces in the 12th century marked the end of an era, but its legacy endures in the global spread of ideas nurtured within its walls.

The Roman Empire, inheriting the intellectual traditions of Greece, established public libraries that sought to democratize access to knowledge. Julius Caesar is credited with the idea of creating a public library in Rome, though it was his successor Augustus who brought the vision to life. The libraries of Rome, such as the Bibliotheca Ulpia, served not only as repositories of Greek and Latin texts but also as spaces for public education and civic engagement. Unlike the exclusive libraries of earlier civilizations, these institutions reflected the Roman ideal of knowledge as a public good, accessible to citizens and integral to the functioning of society. However, the fall of the Roman Empire and the subsequent fragmentation of Europe led to the decline of these libraries, with much of their collections lost or dispersed.

In the Islamic Golden Age, libraries reached new heights of sophistication and inclusivity. The House of Wisdom in Baghdad, established in the 8th century CE under the Abbasid Caliphate, became a global center for translation, preservation, and innovation. Texts from Greece, India, Persia, and beyond were translated into Arabic, creating a repository of knowledge that spanned disciplines and cultures. Scholars at the House of Wisdom not only preserved ancient texts but also advanced them, making original contributions in fields like astronomy, algebra, and medicine. The collaborative spirit of the institution exemplified the idea of libraries as living entities, where knowledge was not static but constantly evolving.

The legacy of ancient libraries is evident in the modern world, where the principles of preservation, accessibility, and intellectual exchange continue to define the role of libraries. While the mediums have changed—from clay tablets and papyrus scrolls to digital databases—the underlying mission remains constant: to safeguard humanity's collective knowledge and make it available for future generations. The ancient libraries, with their triumphs and tragedies, remind us of the enduring value of learning and the perpetual need to protect it. They stand as monuments to the human pursuit of understanding, a pursuit that transcends time and geography.

CHAPTER 5: MEDICINE AND SCIENCE IN THE ANCIENT WORLD

Herbal Remedies and Natural Healing

The ancient world was deeply intertwined with nature, and healing practices often reflected a profound understanding of the plants, minerals, and natural elements that surrounded early civilizations. Long before scientific methodologies formalized the study of medicine, herbal remedies and natural healing formed the foundation of healthcare. These techniques, passed down through oral traditions and early texts, were rooted in observation, experimentation, and the accumulated wisdom of generations. Whether in the dense forests of India, the deserts of Egypt, or the temperate landscapes of Greece, ancient peoples turned to their environments for solutions to ailments, creating systems of healing that resonate in modern medicine.

The use of herbal remedies dates back tens of thousands of years, as evidenced by archaeological discoveries of medicinal plants in Neanderthal burial sites. This suggests that even our early human ancestors recognized the therapeutic potential of plants. Over time, as societies grew more complex, so too did their approaches to healing. In Mesopotamia, some of the earliest written records of herbal medicine were inscribed onto clay tablets in cuneiform script. These texts often combined spiritual and medicinal practices, reflecting a worldview in which health and illness were inseparable from the divine. Remedies included ingredients such as poppy, which was used to alleviate pain, and juniper, valued for its antiseptic properties. These treatments were typically administered in conjunction with prayers or rituals, highlighting the holistic approach to healing that characterized many ancient cultures.

In ancient Egypt, herbal medicine was a cornerstone of healthcare, practiced by priests and physicians alike. Papyrus scrolls such as the Ebers Papyrus, dating to around 1550 BCE, provide detailed accounts of treatments for a wide range of ailments. The Egyptians employed a vast pharmacopoeia, including garlic for cardiovascular health, aloe vera for skin conditions, and honey as an antimicrobial agent. Their remedies were often compounded with precision, combining multiple ingredients to enhance efficacy. Egyptian medicine also emphasized preventative care, with dietary guidelines and hygienic practices designed to maintain balance within the body. The integration of herbal remedies with spiritual and practical knowledge made Egyptian medicine highly influential, informing the practices of neighboring cultures.

The Indian subcontinent developed one of the most sophisticated systems of natural healing in the form of Ayurveda, a tradition that dates back over 3,000 years. Ayurveda, meaning "the science of life," is grounded in the belief that health is achieved through harmony between the body, mind, and environment. Herbal remedies are central to this system, with plants like turmeric, ashwagandha, and holy basil playing prominent roles. These herbs were not only used to treat specific conditions but also to promote overall well-being and longevity. Ayurvedic texts, such as the Charaka Samhita and Sushruta Samhita, codified this knowledge, detailing the properties of thousands of plants and their applications. Ayurveda's emphasis on individualized treatment, taking into account factors such as constitution and lifestyle, reflects a nuanced understanding of health that remains relevant today.

In ancient China, herbal medicine was similarly integrated into a broader framework of health and philosophy. Traditional Chinese Medicine (TCM), which emerged during the Shang Dynasty and gained prominence in the Han Dynasty, emphasizes the balance of yin and yang and the flow of qi, or life energy. Herbs were categorized according to their energetic properties, such as warming or cooling, as well as their effects on specific organ systems. Ginseng, for example, was prized for its ability to restore vitality, while licorice root was used to harmonize other ingredients in herbal formulas. The Chinese pharmacopoeia, as documented in texts like the Shennong Bencao Jing, included not only plants but also minerals and animal products, reflecting a comprehensive approach to natural healing.

The Greeks, heavily influenced by Egyptian and Mesopotamian practices, made significant contributions to the understanding of herbal medicine. Hippocrates, often regarded as the father of medicine, advocated for treatments based on careful observation and natural remedies. His emphasis on diet, exercise, and herbal therapies laid the foundation for Western medicinal traditions. Theophrastus, a student of Aristotle, further advanced the study of plants in his work "Enquiry into Plants," systematically describing their properties and uses. The Roman physician Galen built upon these traditions, compiling extensive texts that would dominate medical thought for centuries. Roman medicine, like that of Greece, relied heavily on herbs such as rosemary, fennel, and sage, which were cultivated in gardens and used for their therapeutic benefits.

The Islamic Golden Age saw the preservation and expansion of ancient herbal knowledge, as scholars translated Greek, Roman, and Indian medical texts into Arabic. Figures like Avicenna (Ibn Sina) synthesized this knowledge with their own observations, creating comprehensive works such as "The Canon of Medicine." This text, widely studied in Europe during the Middle Ages, included detailed descriptions of herbs and their applications. Islamic physicians also introduced new plants and treatments to the Mediterranean world through trade and exploration, enriching the global pharmacopoeia.

Throughout the ancient world, herbal remedies were deeply tied to cultural practices and beliefs. Healing was not only a physical process but also a spiritual and social one, involving rituals, prayers, and community support. While the effectiveness of some ancient remedies has been validated by modern science, others were likely placebos or based on symbolic associations. For example, the doctrine of signatures—a belief that a plant's appearance indicated its medicinal use—led to the use of liverwort for liver ailments and eyebright for eye conditions. Though not always scientifically accurate, such practices reveal the creativity and resourcefulness of ancient healers.

The legacy of herbal medicine endures in contemporary healthcare, where many modern drugs are derived from plant compounds. Aspirin, for instance, originates from salicylic acid found in willow bark, a remedy used by ancient cultures for pain relief. Similarly, the antimalarial drug quinine was derived from the bark of the cinchona tree, long utilized by indigenous peoples of South America. Even as synthetic pharmaceuticals dominate modern medicine, the resurgence of interest in natural remedies and holistic health reflects an enduring connection to ancient traditions.

The art of healing with herbs is a testament to humanity's ability to learn from nature and adapt its wisdom to meet the challenges of illness and disease. It is a story of observation, trial and error, and the relentless pursuit of well-being. The ancient healers, with their intimate knowledge of the natural world, laid the groundwork for the medical advancements we benefit from today. Their legacy, preserved in texts, traditions, and practices, continues to inspire and inform the ongoing quest to understand and harness the healing power of nature.

The Roots of Modern Surgery in Ancient Practices

The development of surgery in the ancient world reveals a remarkable blend of ingenuity, courage, and the relentless pursuit of knowledge. Long before the advent of modern anesthesia, sterilization, or advanced surgical tools, ancient physicians were performing procedures that laid the groundwork for contemporary medical practices. Rooted in necessity, innovation, and an evolving understanding of human anatomy, these early surgical techniques reflect the resourcefulness of healers who sought to alleviate suffering and save lives, often under challenging and perilous circumstances. The roots of modern surgery can be traced to civilizations that approached the human body not only as a vessel of life but as a complex system that could be repaired, altered, or healed through intervention.

In ancient Egypt, the art of surgery was deeply intertwined with religious and medical practices. Egyptian physicians, who were often priest-healers, performed surgical procedures as part of their broader medical repertoire. The Edwin Smith Papyrus, a 3,600-year-old medical text, provides a detailed account of surgical techniques and case studies, showcasing the Egyptians' advanced understanding of trauma and anatomy. This document outlines methods for treating fractures, dislocations, and wounds, including instructions for cleaning and dressing injuries. The use of honey, valued for its antimicrobial properties, and linen bandages reflects an early understanding of infection control. Egyptian surgeons also practiced trepanation, a procedure involving the removal of a section of the skull, often to relieve pressure or treat head injuries. While the risks were significant, the survival of patients attests to the skill and precision of these early practitioners.

The Indian subcontinent contributed significantly to the advancement of surgical knowledge, particularly through the work of Sushruta, often regarded as the father of surgery. Sushruta's seminal text, the "Sushruta Samhita," composed around the 6th century BCE, is a comprehensive treatise on medicine and surgery. It describes a wide range of procedures, from cataract removal to complex reconstructive surgeries, including rhinoplasty. The latter, developed as a response to the cultural practice of punishing criminals by amputating their noses, demonstrates the practical and innovative spirit of ancient Indian surgery. Sushruta also emphasized the importance of anatomical knowledge, advocating for the dissection of human and animal bodies to better understand the structures and functions of tissues and organs. His meticulous descriptions of surgical instruments, many of which resemble modern tools, highlight the sophistication and foresight of ancient Indian surgical practices.

In ancient China, surgical procedures were less emphasized compared to herbal medicine and acupuncture, yet they were not absent. Traditional Chinese Medicine viewed the body as an interconnected system of energy pathways, and surgical intervention was often seen as a last resort.

However, records from the Han Dynasty describe the use of surgical techniques to treat severe injuries and abscesses. Hua Tuo, a renowned physician of the 2nd century CE, is credited with pioneering the use of anesthesia in surgery. He developed a herbal anesthetic mixture called "mafeisan," which reportedly allowed patients to undergo invasive procedures with reduced pain. Hua Tuo's contributions reflect an early understanding of pain management, a critical component of surgical practice.

The Greeks brought a systematic and philosophical approach to surgery, driven by their quest to understand the natural world. Hippocrates, whose teachings form the foundation of Western medicine, emphasized the importance of observation, diagnosis, and minimally invasive techniques. His methods for treating dislocations, fractures, and wounds focused on alignment and stabilization, often employing splints and bandages. Hippocratic surgeons recognized the risks of infection and sought to minimize unnecessary interventions. Building on this tradition, the Hellenistic period saw significant advancements in surgical knowledge, particularly in Alexandria, home to one of the most renowned medical schools of antiquity. There, Herophilos and Erasistratos conducted anatomical dissections and made groundbreaking discoveries about the nervous and circulatory systems. Their work laid the foundation for more precise and informed surgical techniques.

The Roman Empire, inheriting Greek medical knowledge, further refined surgical practices and made them more accessible through military and public health initiatives. Roman military surgeons, stationed with legions across the empire, developed practical and efficient techniques for treating battlefield injuries. Tools such as scalpels, forceps, and bone saws, many of which were crafted from bronze or iron, were standardized and widely used. The Romans also emphasized hygiene, recognizing the importance of clean water and sanitation in preventing infection. The writings of Aulus Cornelius Celsus and Galen, both influential Roman physicians, documented surgical procedures and techniques, preserving a wealth of knowledge that would be transmitted to later generations.

Trepanation, one of the oldest known surgical practices, was performed across diverse cultures and continents, from the Americas to Africa and Europe. Evidence of trepanation dates back as far as 10,000 BCE, with skulls bearing signs of healed openings, indicating that patients often survived the procedure. The motivations for trepanation varied, ranging from the treatment of head injuries and epilepsy to spiritual or ritualistic purposes. The survival of trepanned individuals suggests that ancient surgeons possessed a remarkable understanding of cranial anatomy and the ability to conduct such operations with precision.

The Islamic Golden Age saw the preservation, expansion, and innovation of surgical knowledge. Scholars like Al-Zahrawi, known as Albucasis in the West, revolutionized surgery through their detailed writings and inventions. Al-Zahrawi's encyclopedic work, "Al-Tasrif," became a cornerstone of surgical education in both the Islamic world and medieval Europe. He introduced techniques for suturing wounds using catgut, a material still in use today, and described procedures for treating fractures, amputations, and abscesses. His pioneering work in dental surgery and the development of specialized surgical instruments underscore his contributions to the field.

Despite the remarkable achievements of ancient surgeons, their work was constrained by the absence of modern anesthesia, sterilization, and an understanding of germ theory. Pain, infection, and blood loss were constant challenges, often limiting the scope and success of procedures. Yet, the courage and skill of these early practitioners cannot be overstated. They operated in environments that demanded innovation and resourcefulness, laying the groundwork for the surgical advancements that would follow.

The evolution of surgery from ancient practices to modern techniques is a testament to humanity's determination to overcome physical suffering and extend the boundaries of medical knowledge. The contributions of ancient civilizations, preserved through texts, artifacts, and traditions, continue to inform and inspire contemporary surgeons. Their legacy is not only one of technical achievement but also of compassion and commitment to the well-being of others, a legacy that endures in every operating room today.

Astronomy: Ancient Eyes on the Stars

Ancient civilizations gazed at the night sky not with idle curiosity but with a profound sense of purpose. The stars, planets, and celestial phenomena were not merely distant objects to them but intricate parts of their existence, influencing their calendars, navigation, religious beliefs, and understanding of the cosmos. Astronomy, as one of the earliest sciences, emerged from this interplay of observation and necessity, evolving into a sophisticated discipline that shaped the intellectual and practical frameworks of ancient societies. From monumental observatories to detailed star charts, ancient astronomers laid the groundwork for modern scientific exploration, their legacy etched into the very fabric of human progress.

In Mesopotamia, the cradle of civilization, astronomy began as a tool for agriculture and governance. The priests of Sumer, Babylonia, and Assyria meticulously recorded celestial movements on clay tablets, creating some of the earliest known astronomical records. Observing the cycles of the Sun, Moon, and stars enabled them to establish calendars that regulated planting and harvesting seasons, as well as religious festivals. The Babylonians, in particular, achieved remarkable precision in tracking planetary motion, developing mathematical methods to predict lunar and solar eclipses. Their interest extended beyond practical applications; they saw the heavens as a divine script, interpreting celestial phenomena as omens of events on Earth. The Enuma Anu Enlil, a comprehensive collection of celestial observations and interpretations, exemplifies how closely intertwined Babylonian astronomy was with astrology and theology. In ancient Egypt, the alignment of the stars played a central role in shaping their culture and architecture. The annual flooding of the Nile, essential for agriculture, was closely linked to the heliacal rising of the star Sirius, known to them as Sopdet. This event marked the beginning of their New Year and was a cornerstone of their calendar. Egyptian astronomers also demonstrated their knowledge through the construction of monumental structures like the pyramids, which were aligned with specific stars and cardinal points. The precision of these alignments reflects a deep understanding of the celestial sphere, achieved through centuries of observation. Celestial ceilings in tombs and temples, adorned with constellations and star charts, further reveal the Egyptians' fascination with the heavens and their belief in the stars' connection to the afterlife.

In the Indian subcontinent, astronomy developed as both a scientific and philosophical pursuit. Ancient Indian texts like the Rigveda and the Vedanga Jyotisha contain detailed astronomical references, demonstrating an early understanding of the motions of celestial bodies. By the 5th century CE, Indian astronomers such as Aryabhata had made significant contributions to the field. Aryabhata's work, "Aryabhatiya," proposed a heliocentric model of the solar system and accurately calculated the length of a year. Indian astronomy was deeply intertwined with mathematics, leading to the development of trigonometric methods that enhanced the precision of astronomical calculations. These advancements not only influenced local practices but also traveled westward, shaping the development of Islamic and European astronomy.

Ancient China's approach to astronomy was rooted in its unique cultural and philosophical context. The Chinese viewed the heavens as a mirror of earthly affairs, with celestial events reflecting the harmony or imbalance of the natural order. Astronomers, often employed as imperial officials, meticulously observed the skies to identify omens and advise rulers. Their records, preserved in historical texts like the "Book of Han," include detailed accounts of comets, supernovae, and solar eclipses. The Chinese also developed sophisticated instruments, such as the armillary sphere and water clocks, to enhance their observations. The Han Dynasty astronomer Zhang Heng is credited with inventing an early seismoscope, demonstrating the application of astronomical knowledge to broader scientific endeavors. The continuity and precision of Chinese astronomical records have provided invaluable data for modern researchers studying long-term celestial phenomena.

In the Mesoamerican world, the Maya civilization distinguished itself with its extraordinary astronomical achievements. The Maya developed complex calendars, such as the Tzolk'in and the Long Count, based on precise observations of the Sun, Moon, and Venus. Their understanding of celestial cycles influenced every aspect of their society, from agriculture and governance to religion and architecture. Mayan observatories, like those at Uxmal and Chichen Itza, were designed to align with celestial events, such as solstices and equinoxes. The Dresden Codex, one of the few surviving Mayan manuscripts, contains detailed astronomical tables that demonstrate their ability to predict eclipses and track planetary motion with remarkable accuracy. The Maya's integration of astronomy into their cultural and spiritual life underscores their sophisticated understanding of the cosmos and its significance to human existence.

The Greeks, building on the knowledge of earlier civilizations, transformed astronomy into a systematic and theoretical science. Pioneers like Thales of Miletus and Anaximander sought to explain celestial phenomena through natural laws rather than mythology. By the 4th century BCE, Eudoxus of Cnidus had developed the concept of celestial spheres, a model that would dominate Western astronomy for centuries. Aristotle and later Ptolemy refined these ideas, culminating in the Ptolemaic system, which posited a geocentric universe with Earth at its center. Ptolemy's "Almagest," a comprehensive treatise on astronomy, became a cornerstone of scientific thought in the Islamic world and medieval Europe. Greek astronomers also made significant advances in instrumentation; Hipparchus, for instance, invented the astrolabe and compiled the first known star catalog, laying the groundwork for future astronomical observations.

The Islamic Golden Age marked a period of extraordinary growth in astronomical knowledge, fueled by the synthesis of Greek, Indian, and Persian traditions. Scholars such as Al-Battani, Al-Sufi, and Ibn al-Haytham advanced the accuracy of star charts, refined the Ptolemaic model, and developed new instruments like the sextant and quadrant. The establishment of observatories, such as those in Baghdad and Samarkand, exemplifies the institutional support for astronomy during this era. One of the most influential works, "The Book of Fixed Stars" by Al-Sufi, meticulously documented the positions and magnitudes of stars, bridging the gap between ancient and modern stargazing.

The influence of ancient astronomy extends far beyond its historical context. The methods and principles developed by early astronomers laid the foundation for the scientific revolution, inspiring figures like Copernicus, Galileo, and Kepler. The transition from geocentric to heliocentric models, the use of mathematical frameworks to describe celestial motion, and the invention of observational tools all trace their origins to the insights of ancient stargazers. Moreover, the cultural impact of astronomy, evident in art, literature, and philosophy, underscores its enduring significance in shaping human understanding of the universe.

The story of ancient astronomy is one of wonder and determination, a testament to humanity's innate desire to explore and comprehend the cosmos. From the priests of Babylon to the philosophers of Greece, from the scribes of Mesoamerica to the scholars of the Islamic world, generations of observers turned their eyes to the heavens, unraveling its mysteries one star at a time. Their legacy, inscribed in texts, monuments, and the very stars they studied, continues to inspire our quest to understand the infinite expanse above.

Mathematics as the Universal Language

Mathematics emerged in the ancient world not as an abstract discipline but as a practical tool to solve real-world problems. It was born from the need to measure, count, and organize, yet it quickly grew into a profound language capable of explaining the patterns and structures of the universe. From the construction of monumental architecture to the regulation of trade and the prediction of celestial events, mathematics formed the backbone of ancient civilizations. Its universality transcended linguistic and cultural boundaries, evolving into a shared framework for innovation and understanding. The ancient world's foundational work with numbers and geometry continues to resonate in modern science, engineering, and philosophy.

In Mesopotamia, the earliest known evidence of mathematical practice dates back to the Sumerians, who developed a base-60 numerical system around 3000 BCE. This system, still evident in how we measure time and angles, reveals the ingenuity of a society seeking order and precision in commerce and administration. The Babylonians, inheriting and refining this system, produced clay tablets that demonstrate sophisticated mathematical techniques, including multiplication, division, and the calculation of square roots. One of the most famous artifacts, the Plimpton 322 tablet, suggests that Babylonian mathematicians understood principles akin to the Pythagorean theorem over a millennium before Pythagoras. Their ability to solve quadratic equations and create complex tables for astronomical predictions exemplifies the practical and theoretical depth of their mathematical achievements.

In ancient Egypt, mathematics served as a cornerstone for monumental achievements and everyday governance alike. The Rhind Mathematical Papyrus and the Moscow Papyrus, dating to the Middle Kingdom, provide valuable insight into their mathematical understanding. Egyptian scribes employed a base-10 numeral system and devised methods for multiplication and division based on doubling and halving. Geometry played a crucial role in their society, as evidenced by the precise measurements of the pyramids and the alignment of temples with celestial events. Surveyors, known as "rope stretchers," used rudimentary tools to redraw property boundaries after the annual flooding of the Nile. These practical applications underscore the Egyptians' reliance on mathematics not only as a tool for infrastructure but as a means of maintaining social and economic stability.

In the Indian subcontinent, mathematics reached remarkable levels of sophistication, deeply intertwined with philosophy and astronomy. The Sulbasutras, ancient texts associated with Vedic rituals, contain geometric principles used to construct altars with precise dimensions and proportions. These texts hint at an early understanding of the Pythagorean theorem, as well as the use of irrational numbers. By the 5th century CE, Indian mathematicians like Aryabhata and Brahmagupta had made groundbreaking contributions. Aryabhata introduced concepts of zero as a placeholder and developed methods for solving linear and quadratic equations. Brahmagupta expanded on these ideas, formalizing rules for arithmetic operations involving zero and negative numbers. Their work laid the foundation for the decimal system, a revolutionary advancement that would later spread to the Islamic world and Europe, transforming global mathematics.

In ancient China, mathematics was deeply practical, driven by the needs of governance, engineering, and commerce. The "Nine Chapters on the Mathematical Art," a comprehensive text dating to the Han Dynasty, illustrates the breadth of Chinese mathematical thought. Covering topics such as land measurement, taxation, and trade, the text combines practical problem-solving with theoretical rigor. Chinese mathematicians developed methods for solving systems of linear equations using matrices, a precursor to modern algebraic techniques. They also advanced number theory, devising algorithms for finding square and cube roots. The invention of the abacus, a tool for performing arithmetic operations quickly and efficiently, reflects the Chinese emphasis on practicality and innovation.

In ancient Greece, mathematics took on a more abstract and philosophical dimension, laying the groundwork for modern mathematical thought. Influenced by the Egyptians and Babylonians, Greek mathematicians sought to formalize mathematics as a deductive system based on axioms and logical proofs. Thales of Miletus, often regarded as the first mathematician, used geometry to calculate the height of pyramids and the distance of ships at sea. Pythagoras and his followers viewed mathematics as the key to understanding the cosmos, exploring relationships between numbers, music, and the natural world. Euclid's "Elements," a comprehensive treatise on geometry, established a systematic approach to mathematics that would dominate for over two millennia. Archimedes, another towering figure, combined geometry with practical applications, inventing devices such as the water screw and war machines while also approximating the value of pi with remarkable accuracy.

The Islamic Golden Age marked a period of extraordinary mathematical innovation, as scholars synthesized knowledge from Greece, India, and Persia. Al-Khwarizmi, whose name gives us the term "algorithm," played a pivotal role in developing algebra as a distinct field of study. His work, "The Compendious Book on Calculation by Completion and Balancing," introduced systematic methods for solving equations and laid the foundation for modern algebra. Islamic mathematicians also advanced trigonometry, essential for astronomy and navigation, and refined the decimal system introduced by Indian scholars. The translation of Greek texts into Arabic and the subsequent commentary and expansion by Islamic mathematicians ensured the preservation and growth of mathematical knowledge, which would later influence the Renaissance in Europe.

The universality of mathematics allowed it to transcend cultural and temporal boundaries, fostering the exchange of ideas between civilizations. The shared pursuit of mathematical understanding illustrates humanity's innate desire to find order and meaning in the world. Each ancient society, drawing from its unique context and needs, contributed to a collective body of knowledge that continues to shape our understanding of the universe.

The legacy of ancient mathematics is not merely a historical curiosity but a testament to the enduring power of human ingenuity. The principles and methods developed thousands of years ago remain at the core of modern science and technology, from engineering and physics to computer science and economics. In every equation solved, every structure built, and every discovery made, the echoes of ancient mathematicians resonate, reminding us of the timeless nature of their contributions.

CHAPTER 6: TRANSPORTATION AND NAVIGATION

The Advent of the Wheel and Its Evolution

The invention of the wheel is one of the most transformative milestones in human history, a leap of ingenuity that reshaped the way people moved, worked, and interacted with their environment. While seemingly simple in its design, the wheel embodies a profound understanding of mechanical principles and problem-solving. Its origins are deeply rooted in human necessity, born from the need to transport heavy loads and improve efficiency in daily tasks. Over time, the wheel evolved from primitive wooden discs to sophisticated engineering marvels, adapting to the changing demands of societies across centuries and continents.

The earliest evidence of wheel use dates to around 3500 BCE in Mesopotamia, where the Sumerians are credited with its invention. This innovation likely began with the development of sledges, which were used to drag heavy objects across the ground. Over time, the realization that rolling was more efficient than dragging led to the creation of the wheel. These early wheels were solid wooden discs, constructed by fastening planks together and shaping them into a circular form. Initially used for pottery-making, the concept of the wheel was soon applied to transportation, giving rise to the first wheeled carts. These carts revolutionized agriculture and trade, allowing people to move goods and materials over greater distances with less effort.

The wheel's impact on agriculture was profound. Farmers could transport larger quantities of produce, tools, and water, which not only increased productivity but also expanded the scale of farming operations. This, in turn, supported the growth of settlements and the rise of urban centers, as surplus goods could be traded and distributed more efficiently. In Mesopotamian city-states, wheeled vehicles played a pivotal role in the construction of monumental architecture, enabling the transport of heavy stones and building materials. The wheel was more than a tool—it was a catalyst for societal development, facilitating the emergence of complex economies and organized labor systems.

As the use of the wheel spread, its design began to evolve. By around 2000 BCE, spoked wheels appeared in Central Asia, marking a significant advancement in wheel technology. These lighter and more durable wheels were initially used on chariots, which became a powerful innovation in both transportation and warfare. Chariots allowed armies to move swiftly across battlefields, providing a tactical advantage that transformed military strategy. The speed and mobility offered by spoked wheels were unparalleled, and their use spread rapidly to civilizations such as the Egyptians, Hittites, and Greeks. In addition to their military applications, spoked wheels were also used on light carts and wagons, further enhancing trade and connectivity.

In ancient Egypt, the wheel's adoption coincided with the introduction of the horse-drawn chariot during the Second Intermediate Period. These chariots, equipped with spoked wheels, played a crucial role in the military campaigns of the Pharaohs, including those of Thutmose III and Ramses II. Beyond the battlefield, wheeled vehicles facilitated the transport of goods along the Nile, complementing the river's role as a vital trade artery. The wheel's integration into Egyptian society illustrates its adaptability, as it was used in contexts ranging from warfare to commerce and ceremonial processions.

The Indus Valley Civilization, contemporaneous with Mesopotamia and Egypt, also adopted wheeled transportation. Archaeological evidence, such as terracotta models of carts, suggests that the wheel was a critical component of their trade networks. The standardized design of these carts indicates a sophisticated understanding of engineering and mass production. The use of wheeled vehicles allowed the Indus people to engage in long-distance trade, connecting them with regions as far away as Mesopotamia and Central Asia. This exchange of goods and ideas underscores the wheel's role as a bridge between cultures, facilitating the flow of commerce and innovation.

In ancient China, the wheel was instrumental in agriculture, transportation, and warfare. The development of wooden carts with solid wheels enabled farmers to transport heavy loads of grain, water, and other essentials. The invention of the wheelbarrow during the Han Dynasty further revolutionized transportation, allowing individuals to carry heavy loads with minimal effort. In military contexts, wheeled chariots were used during the Warring States period, providing mobility and tactical advantages on the battlefield. The Chinese also developed advanced wheel designs, such as those used in water-lifting devices and mechanical clocks, demonstrating their ingenuity in applying the wheel to diverse fields.

The Roman Empire refined and expanded the use of wheeled vehicles, integrating them into nearly every aspect of daily life. The construction of an extensive network of roads, stretching across Europe, the Middle East, and North Africa, was designed to accommodate wheeled traffic, enabling the efficient movement of goods, armies, and information. Roman carts and wagons were built with standardized dimensions, allowing them to navigate the empire's roads and bridges seamlessly. The Romans also innovated with the use of iron-rimmed wheels, which increased durability and reduced wear on the roads. These advancements underscore the interplay between the wheel and infrastructure, as each development in one area spurred progress in the other.

In medieval Europe, the wheel continued to evolve, adapting to new challenges and opportunities. The introduction of the horse collar and the development of larger, sturdier wheels enabled the use of heavy plows, transforming agriculture in regions with dense or clay-rich soils. The wheel also played a central role in the industrial revolution of the Middle Ages, powering watermills and windmills that mechanized tasks such as grinding grain and pumping water. These innovations highlight the wheel's versatility, as it was applied not only to transportation but also to energy production and mechanical engineering.

The wheel's journey is a testament to human ingenuity and adaptability. What began as a simple solution to the problem of moving heavy objects evolved into a cornerstone of technological and societal progress. Its applications transcended transportation, influencing agriculture, warfare, industry, and even art. The wheel's ability to adapt to the needs of different cultures and eras underscores its enduring relevance, a symbol of innovation that continues to shape the modern world. Its legacy is not merely one of utility but of transformation, as it enabled humanity to move forward—literally and figuratively—into new realms of possibility.

Ancient Ships and the Birth of Global Trade

The advent of ancient ships revolutionized human civilization, connecting distant lands, fostering cultural exchanges, and giving rise to the earliest forms of global trade. Waterways became the lifelines of commerce, enabling societies to transport goods more efficiently than ever before. These vessels, crafted with ingenuity and adapting to the demands of their environment, were not just tools of trade but symbols of exploration, ambition, and the unrelenting human desire to reach beyond the horizon. From the reed boats of Mesopotamia to the grand triremes of the Mediterranean, ancient ships shaped the trajectory of economies and civilizations, laying the foundation for the interconnected world we know today.

The story of ancient ships begins with the simplest of designs. In Mesopotamia, where the Tigris and Euphrates rivers flowed through the cradle of civilization, small reed boats were among the earliest watercraft. Constructed using tightly bound bundles of reeds coated with bitumen for waterproofing, these vessels were light and maneuverable, ideal for navigating rivers and canals. They played a vital role in the region's economy, transporting agricultural produce, pottery, and textiles between city-states. The rivers, acting as arteries of trade, connected settlements and enabled the exchange of goods and ideas. As trade networks expanded, larger and more durable boats, made from wood, replaced the reed craft, opening up routes along the Persian Gulf and beyond.

In ancient Egypt, the Nile was not just a river; it was the lifeblood of the kingdom. Egyptian ships, crafted from acacia or cedar wood, were essential for transporting goods, people, and even colossal stones for the construction of temples and pyramids. The design of these vessels evolved over centuries, from simple dugout canoes to sophisticated sailing ships that harnessed the power of the wind. The Egyptians were among the first to use sails, allowing their ships to travel both downstream with the current and upstream against it. Trade expeditions ventured far along the Nile and into the Red Sea, bringing back valuable commodities like incense, ebony, and gold from the land of Punt. Egyptian ships became symbols of wealth and power, as evidenced by the elaborate depictions in tombs and temples.

The Mediterranean Sea gave rise to some of the most advanced shipbuilding traditions of the ancient world. The Minoans of Crete, one of the earliest maritime powers, constructed sleek, agile ships designed for both trade and exploration. Their vessels, adorned with colorful patterns and equipped with a single mast and square sail, were key to their dominance of Mediterranean trade routes. The Minoans exchanged goods such as olive oil, wine, and pottery with Egypt, Anatolia, and the Levant, creating a vibrant network of commerce that spread knowledge and cultural influences across the region.

The Phoenicians, often called the master mariners of antiquity, took shipbuilding and navigation to new heights. Based in the cities of Tyre, Sidon, and Byblos along the Levantine coast, the Phoenicians built sturdy, seaworthy ships capable of long voyages across open waters. Their keels and ribbed hulls provided stability, while their use of multiple oars and sails ensured speed and maneuverability. The Phoenicians were the first to venture beyond the traditional boundaries of Mediterranean trade, establishing colonies as far west as Carthage and exploring the Atlantic coasts of Europe and Africa. Their ships carried cargoes of precious dyes, timber, and glass, commodities that became highly sought after in distant markets. The Phoenicians' expertise in navigation, guided by the stars and primitive charts, set the stage for future exploration.

In the Aegean, the Greeks transformed shipbuilding into an art and science. Their triremes, warships propelled by three rows of oarsmen, were marvels of engineering, capable of achieving remarkable speed and agility. While primarily designed for naval combat, Greek ships also played a crucial role in commerce, ferrying goods such as olive oil, wine, and ceramics to markets across the Mediterranean and Black Sea. The Greeks' mastery of maritime trade fostered the growth of city-states like Athens and Corinth, whose economies thrived on the wealth generated by shipping. The sea was central to Greek identity, inspiring myths, poetry, and philosophy that celebrated the spirit of exploration.

In the Indian Ocean, the ancient mariners of the Indus Valley, Arabia, and South Asia developed ships suited to the challenges of open-sea navigation. The dhow, a vessel with a characteristic lateen sail, emerged as a versatile and durable design, ideal for harnessing the monsoon winds that dictated the rhythm of trade. These ships connected the ports of India, Mesopotamia, and East Africa, creating a vast maritime network. Archaeological evidence, such as the discovery of ancient dockyards at Lothal in the Indus Valley, highlights the sophistication of their maritime infrastructure. Indian ships carried spices, textiles, and gemstones to eager buyers, while returning with ivory, gold, and exotic woods.

In East Asia, Chinese shipbuilders crafted junks, vessels renowned for their stability and adaptability. Featuring watertight compartments and balanced lug sails, junks were ideal for both riverine and oceanic navigation. During the Han Dynasty, these ships facilitated trade along the Maritime Silk Road, linking China to Southeast Asia, India, and beyond. The exchange of silk, porcelain, and tea for spices, pearls, and precious metals enriched the economies and cultures of all involved. Chinese innovation in shipbuilding, including the use of rudders for steering, influenced maritime practices across the ancient world.

The integration of maritime trade into the fabric of ancient societies cannot be overstated. Ships became the vehicles of cultural exchange, spreading languages, religions, and technologies across continents. The goods they carried—amber from the Baltics, tin from Britain, spices from India, and silk from China—wove a tapestry of interconnected economies. Ports and harbors became bustling hubs of activity, where merchants, sailors, and craftsmen mingled, forging bonds that transcended borders.

Ancient ships were more than just tools of commerce; they were emblems of human ingenuity and ambition. They carried explorers into uncharted waters, traders into foreign lands, and armies into distant conflicts. Their evolution reflects the adaptability and creativity of the civilizations that built them, as well as the enduring human desire to connect, trade, and discover. The legacy of these vessels lives on, not only in the archaeological remnants of their construction but in the spirit of exploration and innovation that continues to drive humanity forward across the seas.

Mapping the Stars for Navigation

For ancient civilizations, the stars were more than just distant, twinkling lights in the night sky. They were a compass, a map, and a guide through the uncharted expanses of land and sea. Long before the invention of magnetic compasses or GPS, human ingenuity turned to the heavens for navigation, unlocking the secrets of celestial patterns to chart courses across vast distances. This reliance on the stars was not merely a matter of convenience but a critical skill for survival, trade, and exploration. Mapping the stars for navigation became one of humanity's earliest and most profound scientific achievements, bridging the gap between observation and utility, and forging a connection between the terrestrial and the cosmic.

The earliest evidence of celestial navigation comes from prehistoric times when ancient peoples began observing the predictable movements of the stars, the Sun, and the Moon. These observations were not random; they were born of necessity. For hunter-gatherers and early agricultural societies, understanding the heavens meant determining the changing seasons, predicting weather patterns, and marking the passage of time. Over millennia, this knowledge evolved into a sophisticated system of navigation, as people began to recognize that certain stars or constellations could serve as fixed points in the night sky, unchanging and reliable guides for orientation.

In Mesopotamia, one of the cradles of civilization, the Sumerians and Babylonians meticulously studied the heavens, recording their findings on clay tablets. They identified constellations and tracked the movements of celestial bodies with remarkable precision. The Babylonians, in particular, created star catalogs that listed the positions of key stars and their relationship to the horizon. This knowledge was essential for both land and river navigation. Merchants traveling along the Tigris and Euphrates rivers relied on the stars to guide their journeys, ensuring safe passage between city-states. Beyond practical applications, the stars held deep cultural and religious significance, as they were often associated with gods and myths, further underscoring their central role in Mesopotamian society.

In ancient Egypt, the stars were equally vital. For the Egyptians, the Nile River served as the lifeline of their civilization, and its predictable flooding was tied to celestial events. The heliacal rising of the star Sirius heralded the annual inundation, marking the start of the agricultural calendar. This profound connection between the stars and the rhythms of life extended to navigation. Egyptian sailors used the stars to traverse the Nile and venture into the Red Sea. The constellations, such as Orion and the Big Dipper, became familiar markers in the night sky, guiding their boats through the dark. Egyptian priests and astronomers, working in temples and observatories, refined star charts and passed their knowledge to future generations, ensuring that celestial navigation remained a cornerstone of their culture.

The Phoenicians, renowned as master mariners of the ancient Mediterranean, took celestial navigation to extraordinary heights. Based in the Levant, they expanded their trade networks across the Mediterranean and beyond, reaching as far as the Atlantic coasts of Europe and Africa. Central to their success was their ability to navigate using the stars. The Phoenicians were among the first to recognize the significance of the North Star, Polaris, which remains fixed in the night sky and marks the direction of true north. By aligning their ships with Polaris, they could maintain their bearings over long distances, even in open waters. This skill allowed them to venture far from the coast, carrying goods such as timber, glass, and purple dye to distant markets. The legacy of Phoenician navigation can still be seen in the knowledge they passed to later seafaring cultures, including the Greeks and Romans.

In the Pacific Ocean, the Polynesians developed a remarkable system of celestial navigation that remains one of the most impressive feats of human ingenuity. Without written records, compasses, or sextants, Polynesian navigators used the stars, along with other natural cues such as ocean swells, cloud formations, and bird flight patterns, to travel vast distances between islands. They memorized the positions of specific stars and their rising and setting points on the horizon, creating mental star maps that guided them across thousands of miles of open ocean. These navigators, known as wayfinders, could read the night sky like a map, using constellations such as the Southern Cross to orient themselves. Their voyages, from Hawaii to New Zealand to Easter Island, stand as a testament to their unparalleled skill and understanding of the natural world.

In ancient China, astronomy and navigation were closely linked. Chinese scholars meticulously charted the stars, creating detailed celestial maps that informed both land and sea travel. The Chinese developed a unique system of dividing the sky into constellations known as lunar mansions, which were used to track the Moon's position and guide journeys. By the Han Dynasty, they had also begun using the gnomon, a simple instrument that measured the Sun's shadow to determine latitude. This blending of celestial and solar observations allowed Chinese traders and explorers to navigate the Silk Road and venture into the Indian Ocean, connecting China to the wider world through trade and cultural exchange.

The Greeks further advanced the science of celestial navigation, combining their philosophical inquiry with practical applications. Greek astronomers such as Hipparchus and Ptolemy created detailed star catalogs and developed theories about the motion of celestial bodies. The invention of the astrolabe, an instrument used to measure the altitude of stars above the horizon, revolutionized navigation by providing sailors with a reliable method for determining latitude. Greek sailors relied on these tools and their knowledge of the stars to navigate the Aegean and Mediterranean seas, linking city-states and fostering the exchange of goods and ideas.

The Islamic Golden Age saw a flourishing of astronomical knowledge that greatly enhanced celestial navigation. Scholars such as Al-Battani and Al-Zarqali refined Greek and Indian astronomical models, creating star charts and instruments of unprecedented accuracy. The development of the quadrant and the improved astrolabe allowed Islamic mariners to undertake long voyages with confidence. This expertise facilitated the expansion of trade networks across the Indian Ocean, connecting the Islamic world to East Africa, India, and Southeast Asia. The knowledge preserved and expanded during this era would later influence European exploration during the Age of Discovery.

The mapping of the stars for navigation is a story of human ingenuity, curiosity, and perseverance. From the rivers of Mesopotamia to the vast Pacific Ocean, ancient mariners turned to the heavens to chart their paths, bridging the gap between observation and application. Their legacy lives on in modern navigation, where celestial principles still underpin the tools and technologies that guide us across land, sea, and sky. The stars, constant and unyielding, remain a reminder of the timeless connection between humanity and the cosmos.

Roads and Networks: Building Connectivity

Roads have served as the veins of civilizations, carrying the lifeblood of commerce, communication, and culture across landscapes both rugged and vast. From dirt tracks worn by countless footsteps to the meticulously engineered highways of empires, the development of roads and networks has been an essential force in shaping societies. They connected cities, bridged rural and urban divides, and enabled the movement of armies, goods, and ideas. The construction and maintenance of these pathways not only marked technological progress but also reflected the organizational and political ambitions of the civilizations that built them. The story of roads is one of connectivity, of linking people and places in ways that transformed human history.

The first roads were not built—they were trails carved by instinct and necessity. Early humans and animals followed paths of least resistance, creating tracks through forests, mountains, and plains. These natural trails often led to sources of water, hunting grounds, or rich pastures. Over time, as societies began to settle and develop agriculture, these paths became more defined, connecting villages to fields, pastures, and neighboring communities. The movement of people and goods along these routes was the precursor to more formalized networks, as early leaders recognized the importance of facilitating travel and trade.

In Mesopotamia, the Sumerians were among the first to construct roads with deliberate intent. As city-states like Ur and Uruk grew into bustling hubs of commerce and administration, the need for reliable transportation routes became clear. Sumerian roads were relatively simple, often made of compacted earth or gravel, but they were essential for linking cities with their hinterlands. These roads facilitated the movement of goods such as grain, wool, and pottery, enabling trade between settlements and fostering economic interdependence. The Sumerians also used their roads for religious and political purposes, as they allowed for the transport of offerings, tributes, and officials between temples and palaces.

In ancient Egypt, the Nile River served as the primary highway, but roads played a crucial supporting role. The Egyptians constructed paths to connect the river with quarries, mines, and construction sites. These roads, often paved with stone, enabled the transport of massive blocks used to build pyramids, temples, and monuments. One of the most remarkable examples is the road leading to the Giza plateau, which was used to haul limestone blocks from nearby quarries. The construction of such roads required significant planning and labor, reflecting the centralized authority of the Egyptian state. These pathways were more than utilitarian—they were manifestations of the pharaohs' ability to mobilize resources and manpower on an unprecedented scale.

The Indus Valley Civilization, known for its advanced urban planning, also built roads that demonstrated a high degree of organization. Cities like Mohenjo-Daro and Harappa were laid out in grid patterns, with wide, straight streets intersecting at right angles. These roads, often paved with brick, facilitated the movement of people, carts, and goods within the city and connected urban centers to surrounding regions. The integration of drainage systems alongside the roads highlights the Indus people's holistic approach to infrastructure. Their roads were not just pathways but part of a broader design that prioritized efficiency, hygiene, and accessibility.

The Persian Empire under Darius the Great set new standards for road construction and connectivity. The Royal Road, stretching over 1,500 miles from Sardis in Asia Minor to Susa in Persia, was a marvel of engineering and organization. Built to support the empire's administrative and military needs, the Royal Road allowed couriers to travel its length in just seven days, thanks to a system of relay stations with fresh horses. This network not only facilitated the rapid dissemination of royal decrees but also boosted trade and cultural exchange across the vast empire. Merchants, travelers, and diplomats used the road to navigate the diverse landscapes of the Persian realm, making it a lifeline of imperial cohesion.

In the Mediterranean world, the Romans elevated road construction to an art and science. The Roman road network, stretching over 250,000 miles at its height, was a testament to the empire's engineering prowess and organizational capacity. These roads, built with layers of stone, gravel, and concrete, were designed to endure the wear and tear of heavy traffic and harsh weather. The Roman practice of building roads in straight lines, regardless of natural obstacles, was both a technical achievement and a symbol of imperial determination. Roads like the Via Appia, which connected Rome to southern Italy, served as vital arteries for the movement of legions, merchants, and civilians. Roman roads were not merely functional—they were instruments of empire, enabling the projection of power and the integration of diverse provinces into a unified whole.

In ancient China, the development of roads was closely tied to the growth of the Silk Road, a vast network of trade routes connecting East and West. The Chinese built extensive road systems to facilitate the movement of goods such as silk, tea, and ceramics, as well as ideas, technologies, and religions. The Qin and Han dynasties invested heavily in road construction, creating paths that linked the imperial capital to distant provinces and frontier regions. These roads were often reinforced with stone and equipped with waystations to support travelers and officials. The integration of roads with other forms of infrastructure, such as canals and bridges, reflects the Chinese emphasis on creating a cohesive and interconnected realm.

The Maya civilization in Mesoamerica constructed an impressive network of roads, known as sacbeob, which were paved with limestone and often elevated above the surrounding terrain. These roads connected cities, ceremonial centers, and agricultural areas, facilitating trade and communication across the Yucatan Peninsula. The sacbeob were not only practical but also imbued with symbolic significance, as they were often associated with religious rituals and processions. The construction of these roads demonstrates the Maya's ability to organize large-scale projects and reflects their complex social and economic systems.

Roads and networks in the ancient world were far more than mere pathways; they were the scaffolding of civilizations. They enabled the exchange of goods, the spread of ideas, and the exercise of political and military power. They connected people, fostering collaboration and innovation, while also serving as symbols of authority and ambition. The legacy of these ancient roads endures in the modern world, where the principles of connectivity and infrastructure continue to shape the way we live, work, and interact. Each road, whether carved into the earth or laid with stone, tells a story of human ingenuity and the unyielding desire to bridge distances and build connections.

Chapter 7: Sustainable Practices of the Ancients

Water Management Systems: Wells, Aqueducts, and Reservoirs

Water has always been the essence of life, and ancient civilizations understood this fundamental truth with remarkable clarity. Their survival, prosperity, and expansion depended on their ability to access, manage, and distribute water in ingenious ways. The challenges posed by arid climates, seasonal rainfall, and growing populations spurred the development of sophisticated water management systems. Wells, aqueducts, and reservoirs became the lifelines of ancient societies, embodying their technical innovation, organizational capacity, and intimate understanding of the natural world. These systems not only sustained daily life but also supported agriculture, industry, and urbanization, ensuring the longevity of civilizations that thrived in environments where water was often scarce.

Wells were among the earliest solutions devised by humans to access groundwater. Simple in concept yet transformative in impact, they provided a reliable source of water in regions where surface water was absent or insufficient. The earliest wells, dating back to the Neolithic period, were hand-dug and lined with stones or wood to prevent collapse. In the Indus Valley Civilization, wells became a defining feature of urban planning. Cities like Mohenjo-Daro boasted an extensive network of wells, strategically placed to serve neighborhoods and public spaces. These wells, often cylindrical and lined with carefully laid bricks, demonstrated a keen understanding of engineering principles. Their widespread use ensured that residents had access to clean water, even during periods of drought, and supported the civilization's advanced sanitation systems.

In ancient Mesopotamia, wells complemented the region's extensive irrigation networks. The Sumerians and Babylonians, living in a land defined by its rivers, understood the importance of supplementing river water with groundwater. Wells were often dug in agricultural fields to provide an additional source of irrigation, ensuring that crops could be watered even when river levels dropped. These early farmers developed tools like the shaduf, a simple lever mechanism used to lift water from wells and canals. The combination of wells and surface water systems allowed Mesopotamian societies to cultivate fertile lands and sustain large urban centers, despite the region's harsh climate.

As societies grew and cities expanded, the need for long-distance water transport became evident. Aqueducts emerged as a revolutionary solution, enabling civilizations to bring water from distant sources to urban areas. The ancient Egyptians constructed some of the earliest aqueducts, using canals and raised channels to divert water from the Nile to agricultural fields and settlements. Their understanding of gradients and flow dynamics ensured that water could travel over long distances with minimal loss. These systems not only supported agriculture but also supplied water for domestic use and temple rituals, underscoring the multifaceted importance of water in Egyptian society.

The Romans elevated aqueduct construction to an unprecedented level of sophistication. Their aqueducts, a defining feature of Roman engineering, were marvels of precision and durability. Constructed with materials like stone, brick, and concrete, Roman aqueducts spanned vast distances, often incorporating arches to traverse valleys and bridges to cross rivers. The Aqua Appia, built in 312 BCE, was the first of many such structures that supplied Rome with water from distant springs. Over time, the Romans built an extensive network of aqueducts, supplying cities, baths, fountains, and even private households with a steady flow of water. The sheer scale of these projects required meticulous planning and organization, reflecting the administrative efficiency of the Roman state.

Reservoirs played an equally vital role in ancient water management, storing surplus water for times of scarcity. In regions with irregular rainfall, reservoirs ensured a consistent water supply, supporting agriculture and mitigating the impact of droughts. The Harappans of the Indus Valley Civilization built massive reservoirs, often integrated into their urban planning. The Great Bath of Mohenjo-Daro, while primarily a ceremonial structure, also functioned as a water storage facility, showcasing the dual purposes of such constructions. These reservoirs were meticulously designed, with steps leading down to the water level, allowing for easy access and maintenance.

In ancient India, stepwells represented a unique approach to combining water storage and accessibility. These structures, intricately carved and architecturally stunning, consisted of a series of steps descending to a central water source. Stepwells served both practical and social functions, providing water for drinking, irrigation, and religious rituals while also acting as gathering places for communities. Their design reflected a deep understanding of hydrology, as they allowed water to be collected and preserved even in arid regions.

The Nabataeans of Petra, a civilization that thrived in the arid deserts of what is now Jordan, demonstrated exceptional ingenuity in water management. They constructed an elaborate system of reservoirs, cisterns, and channels to capture and store rainwater. These systems ensured that the Nabataeans could sustain their cities and agriculture despite the harsh desert environment. The integration of water management into their urban infrastructure allowed Petra to become a thriving center of trade and culture, defying the challenges of its surroundings.

In ancient China, reservoirs and irrigation systems were integral to the development of agriculture and the growth of centralized states. The Dujiangyan irrigation system, built during the Qin Dynasty, is a testament to Chinese engineering prowess. This system diverted water from the Min River to irrigate vast tracts of farmland, transforming the Sichuan Basin into a fertile and prosperous region. Unlike traditional dams, Dujiangyan used a combination of weirs and canals to control water flow without disrupting the river's natural course. This innovative approach minimized flooding while ensuring a stable water supply, benefiting generations of farmers and enabling the region's economic expansion.

The integration of wells, aqueducts, and reservoirs into ancient societies was not just a matter of engineering—it was a reflection of cultural values and priorities. Water was often seen as a sacred resource, essential not only for physical sustenance but also for spiritual and communal well-being. Rituals and ceremonies were frequently centered around water, and the structures that managed it were imbued with symbolic significance. The collaboration required to build and maintain these systems fostered a sense of collective responsibility, uniting communities in their shared reliance on a precious resource.

The legacy of ancient water management systems endures in the modern world, where the principles they established continue to inform contemporary practices. Their ingenuity and adaptability serve as reminders of the profound connection between humanity and the natural world. By studying these systems, we gain not only an appreciation for the achievements of the past but also valuable insights into addressing the water challenges of the present and future. The wells, aqueducts, and reservoirs of antiquity stand as enduring testaments to the resourcefulness and resilience of the civilizations that built them.

Renewable Energy: Wind, Water, and Early Power Systems

Harnessing the natural forces of wind and water marked a pivotal moment in human history, as ancient civilizations sought innovative ways to meet their growing needs for energy. Long before industrialization, people understood that nature's endless rhythm could be transformed into power, providing them with the means to grind grain, irrigate fields, and transport goods. These early systems were not only remarkable feats of engineering but also a testament to humanity's ability to adapt and innovate in harmony with the environment. By utilizing renewable energy sources, these societies laid the groundwork for technologies that would influence generations to come, while demonstrating a sustainable relationship with their surroundings.

The earliest evidence of wind-powered technology can be traced to ancient Persia, where windmills were used as early as 500–900 CE to grind grain and pump water. These vertical-axis windmills were simple yet effective, consisting of a central shaft connected to sails made of reed or fabric. Positioned in wind-rich regions, they harnessed the steady gusts sweeping across the arid landscapes. The energy produced by these windmills alleviated the labor-intensive process of grinding by hand and provided a consistent water supply for irrigation in areas where rainfall was sparse. The ingenuity of Persian windmills lay not only in their mechanical efficiency but also in their adaptability to the region's environment, demonstrating an early understanding of sustainable energy use.

In the Mediterranean, wind power found its way into the maritime world. Ancient sailors, particularly the Greeks and Phoenicians, relied on the wind to propel their ships across vast distances. The design of sails evolved over time, from simple square shapes to more advanced triangular configurations that allowed for greater maneuverability and control. These innovations enabled trade networks to flourish, connecting distant regions and fostering cultural exchange. The reliance on wind energy for navigation was not merely a practical necessity but also a profound realization of nature's capabilities. By understanding the patterns of prevailing winds and seasonal shifts, these mariners transformed an unpredictable force into a reliable ally.

Water, another inexhaustible source of energy, played an equally significant role in powering ancient societies. The earliest known water wheels appeared in Mesopotamia and Egypt around the 4th century BCE. These devices, often used for irrigation, consisted of a simple wheel fitted with buckets or paddles that captured the kinetic energy of flowing rivers. As the wheel turned, it lifted water from the river and directed it into canals, providing a steady flow for agricultural fields. In the dry and unpredictable climates of these regions, the ability to control water distribution was revolutionary. It ensured crop stability and allowed for the cultivation of larger plots of land, supporting growing populations and urban centers.

The Greeks refined the concept of the water wheel, developing horizontal and vertical designs for a variety of tasks. By the 3rd century BCE, Greek engineers were using water wheels to power mills for grinding grain into flour. These mills became an essential part of daily life, reducing the labor required for food production and increasing efficiency. One notable example is the mill complex at Barbegal in southern Gaul, an impressive Roman installation that utilized a series of water wheels to produce flour on an industrial scale. The operation of such mills reflected not only technical sophistication but also the integration of renewable energy into the economic and social fabric of the time.

In China, water power reached new heights of innovation. During the Han Dynasty, engineers developed the noria, a type of water wheel designed to lift water for irrigation and urban use. These devices were often massive, with wooden or bamboo paddles that scooped water into elevated channels as the wheel rotated. Powered by river currents, norias provided a continuous and sustainable water supply, enabling the expansion of agriculture and the growth of cities. Chinese inventors also experimented with water-driven machinery for industrial purposes, such as bellows for iron smelting and trip hammers for grain processing. These early applications of water power highlight the Chinese emphasis on efficiency and sustainability in their technological advancements.

In medieval Europe, the proliferation of water mills marked a turning point in the use of renewable energy. By the 12th century, water mills were widespread across the continent, powering a variety of industries beyond agriculture. They were used to saw timber, crush ore, and even produce textiles. The adaptability of water wheels to different tasks made them indispensable to medieval economies. Rivers and streams became hubs of activity, with mill towns springing up along their banks. The careful management of water resources, including the construction of dams and channels, ensured the longevity of these systems and underscored the importance of renewable energy in sustaining economic growth.

Wind power also gained prominence in medieval Europe, particularly with the introduction of horizontal-axis windmills in the 12th century. These windmills, which originated in northern Europe, featured large blades mounted on a central tower that could be rotated to face the wind. They were primarily used for grinding grain and draining water from low-lying lands, such as the polders of the Netherlands. The design of these windmills evolved over time, incorporating features like adjustable sails and gearing mechanisms to improve efficiency. Their widespread use in agriculture and land reclamation demonstrated the adaptability of wind power to diverse geographical and economic contexts.

The adoption of renewable energy systems in ancient and medieval societies was not merely a response to necessity but a reflection of their resourcefulness and ingenuity. By harnessing the natural forces of wind and water, these civilizations developed technologies that were both efficient and sustainable. They understood the importance of working with, rather than against, the environment, a lesson that resonates strongly in today's world. The legacy of these early power systems lies not only in their technological achievements but also in the principles they embody—principles of balance, innovation, and respect for nature.

These ancient systems remind us of the enduring potential of renewable energy. They were the forerunners of modern wind turbines and hydroelectric dams, proving that sustainable practices have deep roots in human history. Their success was built on the ability to observe, adapt, and innovate, qualities that continue to drive progress in the pursuit of clean and sustainable energy today. The windmills and water wheels of the past may no longer be in use, but their impact endures, shaping the way we think about energy and our relationship with the natural world.

Recycling in Ancient Societies

Recycling, often thought of as a modern response to environmental challenges, has roots that stretch deep into ancient history. Long before industrialized societies began grappling with the consequences of mass production and waste, ancient civilizations developed methods to reuse materials out of necessity, ingenuity, and a respect for limited resources. Recycling in these societies wasn't simply a conscious effort to reduce waste; it was a way of life, embedded in the rhythms of daily existence. Materials were precious, labor was valued, and the concept of discarding something without repurposing it was unthinkable in many ancient cultures. The practices they developed, born from scarcity and practicality, were the foundation of sustainable resource management.

In ancient Mesopotamia, recycling was an intrinsic part of urban life. With cities like Ur and Babylon rapidly growing, resources such as metal and clay were in constant demand. Archaeological evidence shows that broken pottery, or "sherds," was often repurposed rather than discarded. These fragments were used as writing surfaces for receipts, contracts, and other temporary records. The abundance of these clay shards within ancient ruins speaks to their secondary use as a practical and ubiquitous material. Metal recycling was also a common practice. In a region where metals like bronze and copper were both valuable and scarce, broken tools, damaged weapons, and other scrap were melted down and re-forged into new items. This cycle of reuse ensured that valuable resources were not wasted and could be redirected to meet the demands of the community.

The ancient Egyptians similarly embraced recycling, particularly when it came to construction materials. Temples, monuments, and tombs, while built with great care, were often sources of reusable stone for later projects. In periods of economic or political change, rulers would dismantle older structures to repurpose their materials for new buildings, sometimes incorporating the original carvings or inscriptions into their designs. This practice, while sometimes criticized for erasing historical records, was a pragmatic response to the challenges of acquiring fresh building materials. Papyrus, the writing medium of ancient Egypt, was another example of resourcefulness. While new papyrus sheets were produced for important documents, less critical texts were sometimes written on washed and reused sheets, demonstrating a careful approach to conserving resources.

In the Mediterranean world, the Greeks and Romans both demonstrated a keen awareness of material reuse. Roman construction, in particular, showcased the practical application of recycling on a grand scale. Buildings that had outlived their purpose were often stripped of their marble facades, columns, and bricks, which were then incorporated into new structures. The Colosseum itself bears evidence of such practices, as sections of its stone were removed over centuries to supply other construction projects. Roman glassware was another area where recycling flourished. Broken glass was collected, melted down, and re-blown into new vessels. This process not only saved resources but also reduced the need for raw materials, which were expensive and labor-intensive to extract.

The recycling of organic materials was even more widespread and essential. Agricultural societies across the ancient world understood the value of composting long before the term existed. Farmers in ancient China, for example, mastered the art of returning organic waste—such as crop residues, animal manure, and food scraps—back to the soil to maintain fertility and sustain crop production. This cyclical process of renewal ensured that land could be farmed consistently without depleting its nutrients. Similarly, in Europe and the Middle East, animal bones, after serving their initial purpose, were ground into meal and used as fertilizer, providing essential minerals to the soil. Nothing was left to waste in these agrarian systems, as every material had a role to play in sustaining life and productivity.

In pre-Columbian America, recycling practices were deeply integrated into the cultures of civilizations like the Maya and the Aztecs. The Aztecs, living in the densely populated city of Tenochtitlán, developed a highly efficient system for managing organic waste. Human waste was collected and processed into fertilizer for agricultural fields, while food scraps and other organic matter were composted or fed to domesticated animals. This level of resource management not only kept the city clean but also ensured that the surrounding farmland remained fertile enough to support a large population. The reuse of materials extended to textiles as well. Worn-out clothing and fabrics were unraveled and rewoven into new garments or used as padding and stuffing, demonstrating the value placed on every piece of material.

The people of the Indus Valley Civilization exhibited similar resourcefulness. In cities like Mohenjo-Daro and Harappa, the reuse of baked bricks was common. When buildings were demolished, the bricks were salvaged and reused in new construction projects, reducing the need for fresh production. The importance of recycling extended to metals as well. Tools, ornaments, and broken objects were melted down and re-cast, ensuring that these precious materials were not wasted. Even the layout of these ancient cities, with their carefully planned drainage systems, reflects an understanding of efficiency and resource management that is strikingly modern.

Recycling in ancient societies was not confined to practical or economic considerations; it also carried cultural and symbolic significance. In some cases, objects were repurposed in ways that preserved their original essence while giving them a new function. For example, in ancient Greece, broken pottery was often transformed into ostraka, shards used in the process of ostracism—a form of democratic voting. This reuse of materials imbued them with a political purpose, linking the practical with the symbolic in a way that reflected the values of the society.

The ingenuity of ancient recycling practices lies in their adaptability and efficiency. These societies worked within the constraints of their environments, often facing limited access to raw materials and the challenges of expanding populations. By reusing and repurposing materials, they minimized waste and maximized the utility of their resources. Their practices were not only sustainable but also deeply connected to the rhythms of nature and the cycles of life.

The lessons from these ancient systems resonate strongly today. As modern societies grapple with overconsumption and environmental degradation, the practices of the past offer valuable insights into sustainable living. The resourcefulness of ancient peoples serves as a reminder that recycling is not a new concept but a deeply rooted human tradition. Their ability to see potential in what might otherwise be discarded underscores the timeless importance of conservation and creativity. Through their ingenuity, these civilizations left a legacy of sustainability that continues to inspire and guide us in confronting the challenges of the present.

Lessons from the Past: Sustainability for the Future

Humanity's relationship with the environment has always been one of balance, adaptation, and ingenuity. Ancient civilizations, despite their lack of modern technology, developed sustainable practices that allowed them to thrive in diverse and often challenging environments. These societies understood the delicate equilibrium between human needs and natural resources, crafting systems that prioritized renewal, efficiency, and harmony. Their approaches to sustainability, born from necessity and observation, hold valuable lessons for a world grappling with the consequences of industrialization and environmental degradation. By examining the ways in which ancient peoples lived, worked, and coexisted with nature, we can uncover insights that remain profoundly relevant today. The ancients possessed an acute awareness of the cycles of nature and the finite nature of resources. Agricultural societies, in particular, depended entirely on their ability to work in concert with the land. The Mayans of Mesoamerica, for instance, developed an agricultural method known as milpa, a system of crop rotation and intercropping that allowed them to grow a variety of crops while preserving soil fertility. By planting maize, beans, and squash together, they created a mutually beneficial relationship between the plants. Maize provided a structure for beans to climb, beans fixed nitrogen in the soil, and squash spread across the ground, reducing weeds and retaining moisture. This intricate system not only maximized productivity but also ensured the long-term health of the land, reflecting the Mayans' deep understanding of ecological balance.

In the arid regions of the Middle East, the Nabataeans demonstrated extraordinary ingenuity in water conservation. Living in a desert environment, they constructed an intricate network of cisterns, channels, and terraces to capture and store rainwater. These systems minimized evaporation and ensured a reliable water supply for agriculture and daily life. The terraces, carefully built into the slopes of hills, reduced soil erosion and allowed for the cultivation of crops in otherwise inhospitable terrain. The Nabataeans' ability to thrive in such an environment was a testament to their resourcefulness and their commitment to working within the constraints of their natural surroundings.

Similar resourcefulness can be seen in ancient China, where sustainable practices were woven into the fabric of daily life. Farmers in the Yangtze River Valley utilized a system of integrated agriculture that combined fish farming with rice cultivation. By flooding rice paddies and introducing fish, they created a symbiotic environment. The fish ate pests that would otherwise harm the rice, while their waste acted as a natural fertilizer, enriching the soil. This method not only increased yields but also reduced the need for artificial inputs, creating a closed-loop system that was both efficient and sustainable.

Forests, often seen as inexhaustible, were managed carefully by many ancient societies. In Japan, during the Edo period, the practice of satoyama emerged—a system of land management that balanced human activity with forest regeneration. Villages maintained woodlands for timber, firewood, and other resources, but they did so with strict guidelines to prevent overexploitation. Trees were selectively harvested, and replanting was a communal responsibility. This approach ensured that the forests could continue to provide for future generations while maintaining biodiversity and ecological health.

Marine resources were also managed sustainably in some ancient cultures. The Polynesians, renowned for their seafaring and fishing expertise, developed practices that protected fish populations and ensured long-term food security. They established designated fishing areas and seasonal restrictions, allowing fish stocks to replenish. In some cases, they created fishponds—enclosed areas where fish were bred and harvested in a controlled manner. These practices reflected a deep respect for the ocean and an understanding of the need to balance consumption with conservation.

Recycling and repurposing were integral to sustainability in the ancient world. Societies recognized the value of materials and sought to extend their usefulness. The Romans, for example, recycled building materials on a massive scale. When structures fell into disuse, their stones, bricks, and metals were salvaged and incorporated into new projects. This practice was not only economical but also reduced the demand for new resources. Similarly, organic waste was seldom wasted. In ancient Egypt, animal dung was collected and used as fuel or fertilizer, contributing to a cycle of renewal that minimized waste and maximized utility.

Beyond practical measures, many ancient cultures embedded sustainability into their spiritual and cultural beliefs. Indigenous peoples across the

Americas, for example, often viewed themselves as stewards of the land rather than its owners. This perspective fostered a sense of responsibility and interconnectedness, guiding their actions to ensure that natural resources were preserved for future generations. Rituals and ceremonies often celebrated the cycles of nature, reinforcing the importance of living in harmony with the environment.

The decline of some ancient civilizations serves as a cautionary tale about the consequences of unsustainable practices. The overexploitation of resources, deforestation, and soil degradation contributed to the collapse of societies such as the Easter Islanders and the Maya. These examples underscore the delicate balance that must be maintained between human activity and environmental health. When this balance is disrupted, the consequences can be devastating, not just for the environment but for the societies that depend on it.

The ancient world was not without its challenges, but the solutions crafted by these early civilizations demonstrate the power of ingenuity, observation, and respect for nature. Their practices offer a blueprint for modern sustainability efforts, reminding us that the principles of conservation and resource management are not new. They are rooted in a long history of human adaptation and innovation.

As we face the pressing environmental challenges of our time, the lessons of the past are more relevant than ever. The sustainable practices of the ancients remind us that our relationship with the natural world is a partnership, one that requires care, balance, and foresight. By looking to the wisdom of those who came before us, we can find inspiration and guidance for building a future that honors the interconnectedness of all life and ensures the health of our planet for generations to come.

www.ingramcontent.com/pod-product-compliance
Lightning Source LLC
Chambersburg PA
CBHW071947120726
48001CB00005B/2069